The Communal Dinners of Baltimore

Daria Souvorova

in collaboration with:
Nicolas Charon
Gonzo Beck
Rafael Soldi

Chez Nous

Communal Dinners

*Dedicated with all my love to
Nicolas Charon, who supports all of my
crazy endeavors!*

How we met

It took me a while to make friends in Baltimore. How do you make friends after grad school anyway? I ended up at a Couch Surfing event at Ryleigh's Oyster Bar in Mount Vernon. After some awkward shuffling, we found ourselves around a tall bar table sharing fried oysters and stories of how we came to be in Baltimore. An international community dominated the scene. We were artists, nurses, actors, and students all drawn to Charm City from distant lands and seeking a community. There was Corentin, a French exchange student at Johns Hopkins; Lisa, a Russian programmer working at McCormick Spices; Güneş, a Radiologist at JHU; Gonzo, a world traveler working in the nursing field; and Jade, a nomadic actress with an upcoming show in the area.

Our chatter and accents permeated the air, a mixture of south and north, French, Russian, and Turkish. Before long, another French man appeared. Nicolas had arrived in Baltimore a month prior and was attracted to the quintessential French accent of his countryman. It's funny how even when going out to something new, we are unequivocally drawn to the familiar. I wasn't bowled over by him in the rush of meeting new friends.

Before going our separate directions, our table of strangers decided to see Jade's performance the following week. We met at a restaurant down the street from the theater beforehand. An hour into dinner, the French man appeared; late as would come to be usual. We talked about opera, art, theater and culinary traditions, and the seeming lack of interest in these cultural institutions of our contemporaries. I have always wanted a person to see opera with and that is tough to find here. We all made plans to see Peabody Conservatory's operatic rendition of Mansfield Park. This group of strangers became a cohesive group of friends, bent on artistic and culinary exploration!

We found ourselves gathered around my table on Valentine's Day eating a variety of Italian dishes Gonzo and I took turns making in my tiny 4x6 foot kitchen. Sandwiched between the fridge, oven, and two feet of counter space, it was a snug fit for two cooks, but we made it work! The poor white oven was leveled with some cardboard under two of the legs and featured a banged-up knob that I marked up with sharpies after accidentally stripping off all of the marks and temperatures during a deep cleaning episode. The temperatures were a best guess at this point, but my handwritten mark of "375°F" still seemed to work well for most dishes.

Our collection of strangers found an incredible energy in that tiny kitchen and a shared love for cooking and learning about different cultures. We were immigrants, most of us, and were seeking a connection with others. There are few better points of connection than a table full of delicious food. Every few weeks, we decided to throw some money in a communal pot and teach each other the cuisines of our homelands.

Our group shifts as semesters end and jobs change, but we continue to be a magnet for the many immigrants and explorers of International cultures in Baltimore. As we cherish our old friends and develop new friendships we continue our international dinners, now seeking out new cultures to discover together.

Turns out, I like Nicolas after all. We have been traveling the world, eating, and seeing operas together for two years now. We bought a house in here in Baltimore and with our own hands demolished and built up the kitchen of our dreams that could more comfortably accommodate the 2-10 cooks that would frequent it.

Chez Nous pays homage to the home we have built together and the community we welcome into it.

How to use this book

Chez Nous is both a journal of our experience and a curated inspiration for the beginning of yours. Each chapter is a different cuisine that we have explored. Within each culture, you will find three courses and how the meal was organized. You will also find a game plan on how and when to prepare each dish if you would like to replicate it. *Chez Nous* is organized around the idea of communal meals, so it is always portioned for at least six guests. Feel free to adjust the recipes to your guest count.

The final chapters feature intimate dinners that I have prepared with Nicolas for various celebrations as well as meals for a small group of friends - because not every dinner you throw will have 20 guests in attendance!

To me, seasoning is not an exact science, so adjust your seasoning to suit your palette. After all, cooking is meant to be an adventure not a course in accounting! Anytime you are asked to season, assume it is salt and pepper unless stated otherwise.

I use a convection oven, and many of the breads and baked dishes call for a convection fan. If you do not have a convection oven, simply raise the temperature by 25°F (15°C).

The recipes in this book have varied origins. Some were born out of research, others out of a need to use a certain product before it goes bad. Others still are juvenile experiments that I refined over the past decade. I owe a great debt to the chefs and authors of books that taught me the techniques of these various nations and I hope my variations and interpretations are a credit to that which inspired them.

About the Author

Who taught me how to cook? It wasn't much of a tradition in my little family of immigrants from Belarus. Both of my parents work, and have always worked, long hours, so we have never had a lot of time to spend articulating menus and exploring recipes. But we have always had a respect for food.

When I was a kid, my brother and I spent the summers in the woods with my grandmother while my parents worked. We spent our days running through the forest collecting buckets of raspberries and foraging for mushrooms. These are the privileged hobbies of foodies here but in 1990s in Belarus, this was our sustenance. We ate what we found and we found what we ate. Finding our own food instilled in me the value of having, and the value of not having, although that realization came to me much later. My younger brother and I would gather around the table with my grandmother and she would hand us each a bowl of soup full of mushrooms and perhaps a fish my dad caught on the weekend. It was delicious and smelled of the earth. I have a very visceral memory of eating these soups. This memory was always muddled by another thought, *why did my grandmother watch us lovingly instead of eating with us?* It was not until after we came to America and my grandmother passed that I realized – there was only enough soup for two bowls and she let us eat first to make sure we had enough. This selfless generosity is what taught me how to cook, or at least spurred me to learn. If I couldn't say thank you to her, I would at least live a life that she would be proud of.

Bringing people together has always been the incentive, whether it was my little immigrant family for dinner, or a family of friends, I have always longed for community. In high school, I taught myself how to bake cookies and would bring dozens of individualized baggies to hand out to everyone that I passed in the halls. Baking was my first culinary passion. There is something beautiful about how a person's day can be changed with a loaf of bread or a well-timed cupcake.

I was an awkward kid that needed an aid to communicate. Food was always my aid. Living in New York, I wasn't much of a party girl, so we had cooking parties with a small group of friends. To keep things fresh, I started researching all types of cuisines and logging my recipes in a series of notebooks. These books are stained with butter and ink has bled under egg white spills, but I cherish these volumes and reference them often.

Contents

Chez Nous
communal meals

Love Stories
dinners for two

Three's Company
dinners for curated guests

Weeknight Dinners

Jerusalem

Israeli food seems to demand a communal dinner. Riding off the high of our 18 person Indian feast, we wanted to create dishes that would be easy to share and pass around the table and didn't necessitate 18 sets of silverware. I had just found a wonderful Halal meat market and wanted an excuse to buy a quarter of a lamb. A lamb shawarma gave me a perfect excuse to splurge!

Guests: 14

first course:

Baba Ganoush	11
Tabbouleh	12
Hummus with Lemon Parsley Sauce	13
Scallops, Mussels, Clams, and Prawns with Feta in a Tomato Sauce	15
Malawach	16

main course:

Lamb Shawarma	21
Cod Cakes in Tomato Sauce	23
Herb and Cheese Phyllo Pie	25
Mujaddara	27

desserts:

Sweet Cheese Martabak	30
Orange and Almond Syrup Cake	31
Challah Two Ways	32

The Game Plan

2 days before:

soak chickpeas for Hummus

day before:

4 pm	make Orange Confit
	start Challah dough
4:30 pm	burn eggplant for Baba Ganoush
5 pm	Tabbouleh
5:30 pm	divide Challah doughs, braid and form loaves
5:40 pm	Baba Ganoush, step 2
6 pm	cook chickpeas for Hummus
6:30 pm	bake Challah and finish Baba Ganoush
7 pm	finish Hummus and Lemon Parsley Sauce
	spice Lamb and refrigerate
7:30 pm	Orange Almond Syrup Cake

day of:

11:30 am	Cod Cakes
12:30 pm	Herb Pie
1:30 pm	Mujaddara rice
2:30 pm	put Lamb Shawarma in oven
3:30 pm	Seafood and Feta
4:30 pm	assemble Martabak (bake before dessert course)
5 pm	Malawach
6:30 pm	bake Mussels and Feta

Baba Ganoush

serves 6-10

Baba Ganoush is an amazing dish. I have loved it since my first try at a Middle Eastern joint in Brooklyn as an undergraduate student. Make sure you pierce a couple holes in your eggplants first and burn them directly on the flame of your stove top. Rest them on the grate and turn every minute or so.

1. Burn eggplants over direct flame, 15-20 minutes.
   Allow to cool before scooping out the flesh and smashing with fork.
   Place in colander and squeeze and drain.
   Leave in colander for an hour.
2. Mix pulp, garlic, lemon juice and zest, oil. Stir.
   Season with salt and pepper.
   Rest for one hour for flavors to blend.

baba ganoush:

2 large or 4 medium eggplants

3 cloves garlic, minced

zest of 1 lemon

2 tablespoons lemon juice

1/4-1/3 cup (60-80 mL) olive oil

3 tablespoons chopped parsley

2 tablespoons chopped mint

2 tablespoons tahini or sesame oil

salt and pepper

garnish:

lemon zest

green onions, sliced

Tabbouleh

serves 12-16

1/4 teaspoon peppercorns

1/4 teaspoon coriander

1/4 stick cinnamon

3 cloves

2 rounded teaspoons allspice

1/2 teaspoon cumin

1/4 teaspoon green cardamom
  pods

1/8 teaspoon grated nutmeg

3 medium tomatoes,
  1/4 inch (6 mm) dice

1 shallot, minced

4 tablespoons lemon juice

4 bunches parsley, 1 mm mince

2 bunches mint, 1 mm mince

1/3-1/2 cup (80-120 mL) olive oil

salt and pepper

Tabbouleh requires a lot of chopping, but it is definitely worth it. It freshens up the rest of the meal and can be served alongside the lamb in the main course as well. To be honest, I forgot to add bulgur when I was first making it, no regrets!

1.   Grind first 8 ingredients in spice grinder. Mix together in the order ingredients are listed.
Season with salt and pepper, add more lemon juice if needed.

Hummus with Lemon Parsley Sauce

serves 12-16

This one was a crowd pleaser. Don't be afraid to make the whole batch and save some for later. The recipe as it stands makes enough for two generous serving bowls. Be careful as you add the chilies; it can get a bit spicy with two. The baking soda is not required, but I read that it makes a much smoother paste.

hummus:

1. Day before, soak chickpeas in 5 cups water.
2. Drain, place in saucepan with baking soda. Cook, stirring, for 3 minutes.
   Add water, boil. Cook 20-30 minutes until soft when squeezed.
3. Drain chickpeas. Process into a thick paste in food processor.
   Add tahini, lemon juice, garlic, and 1 1/2 teaspoon salt.
   Slowly drizzle in some water if it is too thick. Blend for a few minutes until smooth.
4. Place in bowl, cover in plastic and refrigerate until ready to serve.

lemon parsley sauce:

5. Mix all ingredients and stir.
   Run through food processor if you want a smoother paste.
6. Serve over hummus with pine nuts and a drizzle of olive oil.

hummus:

2 1/2 cup (500 g) dried chickpeas

3 teaspoons baking soda

10 cups (2.5 L) water

2 1/4 cup (540 mL) tahini paste

1/2 cup (120 mL) lemon juice

salt and pepper

lemon parsley sauce:

small bunch parsley, finely chopped

2 green chilis, finely chopped (1 if you want less spice)

1/3 cup (80 mL) lemon juice

1/4 cup (60 mL) white wine vinegar

2 cloves garlic, minced

salt and pepper

garnish:

4 tablespoons pine nuts, toasted

Scallops, Mussels, Clams, and Shrimp in Tomato and Feta

Serves 12-16

Mozzarella with tomato is amazing, but there is something transcendent in blending salty feta and tomato. This transcendence pairs really well with seafood. I am really glad we splurged for the plump lovely seafood from the market.

1 1/2 cup (360 mL) white wine
8 ounces (225 g) mussel meats
10 ounces (285 g) clam meats
4 cloves garlic, thinly sliced
3 tablespoons olive oil
28 ounces (825 mL) crushed
  tomatoes
3 tablespoons oregano, minced
pinch of sugar
6 ounces (170 g) prawns
1/2 pound (225 g) scallops, halved
5 ounces (140 g) feta, crumbled
salt and pepper
zest of 1 lemon

garnish:
lemon zest
green onions, sliced

1. Boil wine. Add clams and mussels, 2 minutes.
2. Transfer to mesh sieve, reserve juice.
3. Preheat oven to 475°F (245°C).
4. Cook garlic in oil for 1-2 minutes.
   Add tomatoes, clam juice, sugar, and oregano. Season with salt and pepper.
   Add half of lemon zest. Cook 20 minutes.
5. Add prawns and scallops, stir 1-2 minutes.
   Add shelled mussels and clams.
6. Transfer half to oven-proof serving dish.
   Top with half of feta. Repeat with remainder.
   Sprinkle green onion and zest. Bake 5 minutes.

Malawach

makes 8 pieces

8 cups (960 mL) bread flour

1/4 cup (50 g) sugar

1 1/3 tablespoon salt

1 teaspoon baking powder

2 3/4 cups (700 mL) warm water

16 tablespoons unsalted butter

1. Combine the first four ingredients. Add water a half a cup at a time, carefully sprinkling all over. Mix with your hand until it comes together. Add water if needed. Knead into a smooth ball, about 5 minutes. Rest for 10 minutes.

2. Melt butter. Butter a large plate. Divide dough into 8 balls, smear with butter and add to plate. Cover with towel and rest 10 minutes.

3. Butter counter. Roll out the dough into a 20 inch (50 cm) square. Flip and add butter as needed. Butter the top and fold into thirds like a letter. Butter the top. Starting from one end, fold short side like a triangle into the long side. Repeat folding over and over like you would a flag that is being stored, until a multi-layer triangle is formed. Tuck corners under and put back on plate. Repeat. Refrigerate 1 hour.

4. Flour work surface. Roll dough into 10 inch (25 cm) rounds. Don't panic if they are imperfect or one of the layers squeezes out of the side.

5. Heat dry frying pan and fry until the dough browns a bit, 4-5 minutes. Flip and fry a few more minutes until the other side browns too.

What is Malawach? I can only describe it as the progeny of a flaky croissant and a fluffy naan. I have developed a passion for breads of all cultures and have been waiting to give this bread a try. Malawach is an unleavened bread that is rolled out, layered with butter, folded and rerolled to create over a dozen flaky layers. It is traditionally served with grated tomato but went wonderfully with our platter of spreads. The beauty of Israeli breads is that they are passed around the table and torn with your hands.

Lamb Shawarma

serves 12-14

I love lamb! In fact, this whole meal is orchestrated around my wish to roast an entire leg of lamb. Someday I will build myself a giant backyard stove. For now, the lamb had to fit into my largest Staub, so it is served in two pieces. Cooked in the sealed Dutch oven and basted in its juices, the lamb turned out beautifully rich and tender.

marinade:

2 teaspoons peppercorns

10 cloves

1/2 teaspoon green cardamom pods

1/4 teaspoon fenugreek seeds

1 teaspoon fennel seeds

1 tablespoon cumin seeds

1 star anise

1/3 cinnamon stick

1 tablespoon sumac

1 teaspoon ground nutmeg

1/4 teaspoon ground ginger

1 1/2 tablespoon paprika

3 tablespoons sea salt

3 cloves garlic, minced

1/3 bunch parsley, finely chopped

1 lemon, juice and zest

1/2 cup (120 mL) peanut or olive oil

lamb:

6 1/2 pound (3 kg) bone-in leg of lamb

1 1/2 cup (360 mL) hot water

1. Dry roast the first 8 ingredients for 1-2 minutes. Add nutmeg, ginger, sumac, and paprika, 30 seconds. Grind in spice grinder with salt. Transfer to a bowl with all other marinade ingredients.
2. Stab the lamb all over with a short knife, place fat side up in large Dutch oven and rub the marinade all over.
   Cover and rest overnight.
3. Preheat oven to 325°F (165°C). Remove lid and place lamb in oven.
   After 30 minutes add the hot water.
   Baste every hour. Cover with lid after the first hour and a half of baking.
   Bake for a total of 4-4.5 hours.

Fish Cakes in Tomato Sauce

serves 12-16

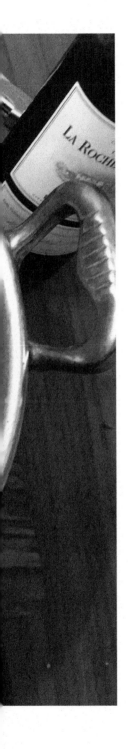

We were already rolling on a theme of fish in tomato sauces so I wanted to continue that into the main course. Our guest list always has at least one non-meat eater so I always strive to include vegetable and fish dishes into the mix. Adding mint to the tomato sauce really brings this dish together for me.

tomato sauce:

1. Heat oil in large pan. Add spices and onion, 8 minutes.
   Add wine, 3 minutes.
   Add tomatoes, chili, garlic, sugar, season with salt and pepper.
   Simmer 15 minutes.

fish cakes:

2. Process bread to form crumbs. Place in bowl.
   Chip fish finely and squeeze out any liquid. Add to bowl.
   Add all ingredients save for olive oil. Form into cakes, 2 inches (5 cm) wide.
3. Heat some oil and fry the cakes in batches. 3 minutes per side.
4. Place cakes in sauce, in one layer if possible.
   Add just enough water to cover the cakes.
   Cover and simmer on low heat for 15-20 minutes.

fish cakes:

4 inch (10 cm) piece of baguette
2 1/2 - 3 pounds (1-1.5 kg) cod/halibut or other white fish fillet
2 medium onions, finely chopped
10 cloves garlic, minced
1/2 bunch parsley, chopped
1/2 bunch cilantro, chopped
2 tablespoons ground cumin
1 tablespoon salt
4 eggs, beaten
4 tablespoons oil, olive or peanut

tomato sauce:

5 tablespoons olive oil
1 tablespoon ground cumin
1 teaspoon paprika
1 tablespoon coriander
2 medium onions, chopped
1 1/2 cup (360 mL) dry white wine
28 ounce (825 mL) can of chopped tomatoes
1 teaspoon crushed chili pepper
3 cloves garlic, sliced thinly
4 teaspoons sugar
handful mint, chopped
salt and pepper

Herb and Cheese Phyllo Pie

serves 12-16

Phyllo dough used to be such a mystery to me, especially since I refused to read the instructions on how to use it. We harnessed it in several recipes in this chapter to delicious results. This is best baked at 400°F (205°C), however, you can put it in with the lamb at 325°F (165°C) and bake it for about 60-75 minutes instead until the top is golden.

1. Preheat oven to 400°F (205°C).
    Pour olive oil in a large Dutch oven or deep heavy pan.
    Add onion and sauté for 8-10 minutes.
    Add celery, 4 minutes.
    Add kale leaves, mix, 4 minutes. Add green onion and herbs, 2 minutes more.
2. Cool and drain in colander, squeeze out as much liquid as possible.
    Place in a bowl and mix in the cheeses, lemon zest, sugar, egg, salt and pepper.
3. Take one sheet of phyllo and brush with reserved oil. Place another on top. I folded them as I went to make the most use of the sheets. You need a stack of 5 high.
    Place a layer on the bottom of a baking dish, cover with the herb mixture.
4. Make another 5 layer stack of phyllo, place on top and tuck in corners.
    Oil the surface.
    Bake for 40 minutes.

filling:

2 tablespoons olive oil
  (more if you didn't reserve the peanut oil from Mujaddara)
1 large onion, diced
1 pound (450 g) kale, stems removed, finely chopped
8 ounces (225 g) celery, thinly sliced
3 green onions, thinly sliced
1/2 bunch parsley, finely chopped
1/3 bunch mint, stems removed, finely chopped
3-4 tablespoons feta (I used what was left over after the Seafood in Tomato Sauce)
1 cup ricotta (240 mL) (reserve the second cup in the container for the Mulabbaq)
6-7 ounces (170-200 g) grated cheddar
zest of one lemon
2 eggs
1/2 teaspoon sugar
salt and pepper

phyllo:

a half a pound (225 g) or so of phyllo dough, 8 full sheets
additional oil, reserved above

Mujaddara

serves 12-16

This is a delicious and filling dish to have on its own, yet it pairs wonderfully with our spiced lamb recipe. If you need to reheat, do not add the fried onions until you are about to serve. You might need to add a bit of water to the lentils and rice to heat it evenly.

2 1/2 cups (500 g) green lentils

7 large onions, thinly sliced

1/3 cup (40 g) all-purpose flour

2 cups (480 mL) peanut oil

2 tablespoons cumin seed

3 tablespoons coriander seed

2 cups (400 g) basmati rice

5 tablespoons olive oil

1 teaspoon ground turmeric

1 tablespoon ground allspice

1 tablespoon ground cinnamon

1 tablespoon sugar

4-6 cups (1-1.5 L) water

salt and pepper

1. Place lentils in saucepan, cover with water. Boil for 15 minutes. Drain and set aside.
2. Mix onions and flour. Season with salt and pepper.
    Heat oil in heavy bottomed pan.
    Fry onion in small batches for 5 minutes or until they turn golden.
    Transfer to a paper towel lined plate.
    Season with salt and pepper.
3. Discard oil (I saved it to brush on the Phyllo sheets for the Herb Phyllo Pie).
    Dry pan and toast cumin and coriander seeds for 1 minute.
    Add rice, olive oil, turmeric, allspice, cinnamon, sugar, about 1 teaspoon salt and some pepper. Stir to coat.
4. Add 4 cups (960 mL) water and lentils.
    Bring to boil, cover, simmer over low heat for 15-20 minutes.
    Add more water as needed.
5. Mix in half the onions and serve topped with remaining onion.

Sweet Cheese Martabak

serves 12-16

This simple dessert will not fail to please. It was my favorite of the evening.

———

cake:

12 tablespoons unsalted butter
10-12 full sheets phyllo pastry,
3 cups (720 g) ricotta cheese
11 ounce (300 g) goat cheese
crushed pistachios, for garnish

syrup:

1/3 cup (80 mL) water
1 1/3 cup (170 g) confectioners
  sugar
1/4 cup (60 mL) lemon juice

1. Heat oven to 450°F (230°C).
   Line shallow baking dish with aluminum foil.
   Make a stack of five or six phyllo sheets, buttering generously in between.
   Place into baking dish, edges should slightly overhang, trim if needed.
2. Blend cheeses and spread all over pastry.
3. Create another stack of 5 buttered phyllo sheets, trim to exact size of baking dish and place over cheese. Roll in edges of bottom dough in to seal the pastry.
4. Butter all over and cut slits almost all the way through in serving sizes.
   Bake about 25 minutes until golden brown.
5. Meanwhile, mix water and sugar and lemon juice, bring to a boil.
   Brush and pour the just boiled syrup over the baked pastry and let absorb.

Orange and Almond Syrup Cake

serves 12-16

Not to insult wheat flour, since I eat bread every minute of the day, but almond flour makes a delicious pastry! This cake pairs well with the rest of the dishes, most of which feature the freshness of citrus juice.

1. Preheat oven to 350°F (180°C). Grease spring form pan with butter.
2. Beat butter, sugar, and zests. Add half of the ground almonds. Add eggs slowly.
   Add remaining almonds, flour, and salt. Add juice of one orange and one lemon.
3. Pour into buttered pan. Bake 50-60 minutes.
4. Place remaining orange juice and sugar in a pan and bring to boil.
   Pour hot syrup over cake immediately after removing from oven. Cool completely.
   Dust with confectioners sugar to serve.

orange almond cake:

14 tablespoons unsalted butter
1 1/2 cup (170 g) confectioners
  sugar + 1/3 cup (40 g) for syrup
zest and juice of two large
  oranges, separated
zest and juice of one lemon
2 1/2 cups (300 g) ground almond
5 large eggs, beaten
3/4 cup (90 g) all-purpose flour
pinch of salt

garnish:

confectioners sugar
orange zest slices

Challah Two Ways:
Seeded and Chocolate with Orange Confit

serves 12-16 each

Challah was my first successful loaf. For the past few years I have been bringing out these loaves for dinners and holiday gifts and as a loaf to cut down for French toast.

———

confit:

1 cup (240 mL) water

1 rounded cup (220 g) sugar

1 orange, seeded, thinly sliced

1. Bring water and sugar to a boil. Set half aside. Add orange to pot, return to boil. Strain out and discard the syrup.
   Add reserved syrup and simmer for 10 minutes. Strain and reserve syrup.

2. Whisk together yeast and water.
   Mix in with flour, eggs, milk, sugar, salt, and butter in stand mixer. Mix on low speed until combined. Medium speed 4 minutes.
   Knead by hand for a few minutes.
   Divide into two balls.

3. Add chocolate and 1/3 cup (60 g) strained confit into one of the dough balls, knead into ball.
Oil both balls and place in large bowls.
Cover and rise in cold oven with pilot light on for 1 hour.

4. Divide each ball into three and roll into plaits. Braid into loaves.
Place on parchment lined sheet, cover loosely with oiled plastic wrap.
Place in lit oven for another hour to rise.

5. Brush egg wash onto each loaf.
Preheat oven to 425°F (215°C) with the convection fan on.
Add seeds to the plain loaf (I used sesame, chia, and coriander seed).
Bake for 20-30 minutes until golden brown and shiny.

dough:
1 cup (240 mL) water
5 teaspoons active dry yeast
7 cups (840 g) bread flour
4 eggs + 4 egg yolks, mixed
1/2 cup (120 mL) milk
1/2 cup (100 g) sugar
1 tablespoon salt
4 tablespoons unsalted butter, melted

filling:
6 ounces (170 g) dark chocolate shards

egg wash:
1 egg and 1 tablespoon water

India

India is a dream for me. I have never been, but very much long to. I love Indian cuisine - the colors of the spices, and the richness that a ginger-garlic masala brings to any dish. Like a university, I always invite more people than my house can hold thinking that only half will show. It seems the call of Indian food tilted the scale and we hosted a group of 18. I found a second table in my studio and guests brought forks and chairs to make it work. We had a wonderful evening full of joy, togetherness, and a half a dozen curries. Gonzo was a guest chef for this evening. In addition to the dishes in this chapter, he created a Chili Fish Curry and a Coconut Sambal for the meal. He did not get me his recipes in time for printing but, with his apologies, will get them uploaded to ChezNousDinners.com!

Guests: 18

The Game Plan

2 days before:

make yogurt if you are making it yourself

day before:

4 pm	Eggplant Dip
5 pm	Cilantro Sauce
5:30 pm	Mint Sauce
6 pm	build Samosas
7 pm	Gulab Jamun
8:30 pm	Mango Lassi

day of:

12 pm	start Goat Biryani - complete all but baking (2 hours)
1 pm	cook Chicken Curry while goat is simmering
2 pm	start Dal Makhani - boil 45 minutes
3 pm	second step of Dal Makhani - 1 1/2 hours, stir occasionally
3:30 pm	make dough for Naan
4 pm	make dough for Chapatis - fry and keep warm
	fry Naan and keep them warm
5 pm	make some basmati rice, according to package instructions
6 pm	bake Goat Biryani
6:30 pm	fry Samosas

Eggplant Curry Dip

serves 8-10

Did I mention how much I enjoy burning eggplant? Here is another opportunity! I wish I made more of this dip for the group but did not buy enough eggplant in advance, so if you are expecting a large group like mine, I would double the recipe.

1. Pierce eggplants in a few spots. Roast over open flame, turning occasionally until blackened and soft, 15 minutes.
Cool, scoop out flesh and mash.
2. Olive oil in heavy bottomed pan. Fry onion for 8-10 minutes.
Add tomatoes 4-5 minutes.
Add ginger, garlic, chili, 2 minutes. Add eggplant, cumin, coriander, and salt to taste.
3. Cover and cook for 5 minutes. Season to taste with salt and pepper. Add cilantro.

2 inches (5 cm) ginger, minced
5 cloves garlic, minced
1 green chili,
   seeded and minced
2 large eggplants
3 tablespoons olive oil
1 onion, finely chopped
2 tomatoes, finely chopped
1 teaspoon ground cumin
1 teaspoon ground coriander
4 tablespoons cilantro, chopped
salt and pepper

garnish:
cilantro

Samosas Two Ways:
Goat with Mint and Curried Potato

serves 16-18

I was really excited about using goat for this dinner. I found a wonderful Halal butcher down the street and wanted to try out goat for the first time! I figured lamb goes well with mint and so would goat. I was right! The potato samosas were inspired by these amazing potato and chicken curry puffs I had in Brooklyn.

goat and mint:

1. Heat oil in large saucepan. Add cumin seeds, fry 1 minute.
   Add onions and fry 8-10 minutes. Add garlic, 2 minutes.
2. Add ground goat, breaking up while cooking, 8 minutes.
   Add ground cumin, coriander, garam masala, ginger, and chili.
   Cook until goat browns.
   Season with salt and pepper and cool.
   Add mint right before building samosas.

curried potato:

3. Boil potatoes until tender.
   Heat oil in pan and fry onion, 8 minutes.
   Add garlic, ginger, chili, 2 minutes.
   Add garam masala, turmeric, and chili powder, 2 minutes.
4. Mash potatoes, add to remaining ingredients. Season with salt and pepper.

build samosas:

5. Preheat oven to 400°F (205°C).
6. Place one sheet of phyllo, brush with melted butter. Stack a second on top.
   Cut horizontally into 3 strips (each 4x10 in/10x25 cm).
7. Make cone shape on one end. Add one tablespoon of filling and roll over itself like a flag. Cut off excess. Stick down with butter.
8. Brush both sides with butter.
   Bake for 15 minutes.

goat and mint:

3 tablespoons oil

2 teaspoons cumin seed

3 onions, finely diced

6 cloves garlic, minced

1 1/2 pound (675 g) ground goat/lamb

1 tablespoon ground cumin

1 1/2 teaspoon ground coriander

1 1/2 teaspoon garam masala

2 inches (5 cm) ginger, minced

1/2 teaspoon chili powder

large handful chopped mint

salt and pepper

curried potato:

1 1/2 pound (675 g) potato, diced

1 cup (175 g) mixed peas, carrots, corn

2 tablespoons olive oil

1 onion, finely chopped

3 cloves garlic, minced

1 inch (2.5 cm) ginger, minced

1 chili, seeded and minced

1/2 teaspoon garam masala

1/2 teaspoon turmeric

1 teaspoon chili powder

2 teaspoons cilantro leaves, chopped

juice of 1/2 lemon

salt and pepper

phyllo:

1/2 pound (450 g) phyllo dough

8 tablespoons unsalted butter, melted

Cilantro Chutney and
Mint and Yogurt Sauce

serves 12-16

We made a lot of bread for this dinner, so we needed a lot of dips with which to eat the bread. Mint and yogurt are a classic combination and a must for an Indian dinner. The cilantro chutney is amazing! I keep it on hand for "emergencies."
It is great with naan or chapati but also beautifully tops salmon or a piece of grilled meat.

cilantro chutney:

1. Grind cilantro in a blender or grinder. Add remaining ingredients.
   Grind into smooth paste.
   Season with salt and pepper and adjust flavors to your liking.

mint yogurt sauce:

1. To make your own yogurt, heat two cups of milk to 180°F (82°C) and keep there for 20 minutes. Cool to 120°F (50°C).
   Mix in 1/4 cup (60 mL) live yogurt. Place in glass jar, wrap the jar in a towel and place in the oven with a pilot light on for 6-12 hours.
   Do not shake or bother it.
   Strain.
2. Mix the remaining ingredients into the strained yogurt.
   Season with salt and pepper.

cilantro chutney:

2 bunches cilantro

1/2 cup (70 g) peanuts

1/4 cup (60 mL) lemon juice

1/3 cup (70 g) brown sugar

1/2 teaspoon ground turmeric

3-4 green chilies

salt and pepper

mint yogurt sauce:

2 cups (480 g) yogurt, Greek or strained homemade

1/2 bunch mint, finely chopped

2 teaspoons sugar

juice of one lemon

salt and pepper

Chapati

serves 16-18

1. Mix the flour and salt in a bowl or on the counter.
    Make a dent in the middle and pour in oil.
    Mix with your hands until the oil is evenly spread out. It will look like wet sand.

2. Add the hot water slowly, mixing in between.
    Add a bit more if needed to bring the dough together into a rough ball.
    Knead the dough for 5-8 minutes until it is smooth.

3. Oil the dough to make it easier to handle and divide into four balls.
    Divide the first three of the four balls into 8 even sections each.
    Divide the last in half. Reserve half for Goat Biryani and divide the second half into 4 balls. You should have 28 small balls and one larger.

4. Flour your counter generously.
    Flatten each ball and roll out into a 4-5 inch (10-13 cm) circle.
    Flip to spread flour around and roll out to an 8 or 9 inch (20 or 23 cm) circle.
    Repeat with remaining chapati.

5. Heat up a dry frying pan or Dutch oven.
    Add one chapati at a time and wait for the edges to turn lighter. Lift up occasionally to check for slight browning. This should take about 30-40 seconds. The surface will begin to make small bubbles. This is good.
    Flip and cook for the same amount of time on the other side.
    Flip back to the first side. Your chapati should start blowing up and making a large bubble. Smash it down and flip and cook for another 10 seconds on the other side.
    Keep warm and covered with foil or a towel to prevent drying out.

This was my first time making chapati. I ate some amazing chapati in Malaysia. For some reason they seemed complicated, maybe it was the foreign name of the flour, but really it is a mixture of white and wheat flour. You will need 3/4 cup (180 mL) of this dough for the Goat Biryani so I would make the full recipe for a large crowd, but feel free to divide in half for a smaller party. I made it in two batches. This will make 28 chapati and the crust. The most exciting part is when the chapati starts to make a giant bubble and blow up, you know it is a success!

———

7 cups (840 g) chapati flour
  (or 3 1/2 cups bread flour and
  3 1/2 cups wheat flour)
1/2 cup (120 mL) olive oil
1 1/2 teaspoon salt
2 1/2-3 cups (600-720 mL) hot
  water

Chicken and Fig Curry

serves 6-8 alone or 14-18 as part of meal

12 dried figs, chopped

2 pounds (900 g) boneless,
    skin-less chicken thighs, chopped

1 1/3 cup (300 mL) of yogurt

3 teaspoons garam masala

2 teaspoons chili powder

salt and pepper

3 tablespoons olive oil

2 large onions, finely diced

1 large cinnamon stick

5 cloves garlic, minced

2 inches (5 cm) ginger, minced

I wanted a sweet curry. Gonzo insists that figs do not belong in traditional Indian cuisine, and I am sure he is right, but I wanted a sweet curry. I am sure I have seen other people doing it. Try it!

1. Combine chicken, yogurt, garam masala, chili powder, salt, and pepper.
    Cover and marinate overnight.

2. Pour boiling water over figs.
    Soak 10 minutes. Drain.
    Add to chicken mixture.

3. Heat olive oil in Dutch oven.
    Add onion and cinnamon, 10 minutes.
    Add garlic and ginger, 4-5 minutes.
    Add chicken, mix and cover. Cook for 15-20 minutes. Stir every few minutes.

Goat Biryani

serves 14-18

This dish is always a crowd pleaser in the Indian joints I frequent. Only once did I see it presented traditionally with the chapati crust. Reading many recipes, I decided this was an amazing challenge to make authentically with a chapati crust and goat meat. You will need a very large Dutch oven to accommodate this dish. I use a 7 quart Staub. I love the oval shaped Staub for this dish because it has the largest surface searing area of any Dutch oven I have found. The crust is very important in this recipe, so don't skip it. If you do, use a very tight sealed lid. The rice is not cooked all of the way through before baking, it finishes cooking from the steam trapped in the dish during baking.

1. Put oil in your large Dutch oven. Sear the goat in small batches until it is golden. Set aside on a plate.
2. Add a few tablespoons of olive oil to the same Dutch oven. Add the onions and cook for 8-10 minutes.
   Meanwhile, grind all of the spices in a grinder. Set aside.
3. Remove half of the onions and reserve for later. Add the garlic and ginger to the remaining onions, 2 minutes. Add the ground spices, turmeric, and chili powder to the onions.
   Stir regularly as the mixture may start to burn a bit. Turn down the heat if needed.
   Add the meat, yogurt, tomato paste and stir. Add 2 cups (480 mL) water. Bring to a boil. Move to a back burner and turn down to lowest simmer. Cover and cook for at least an hour. 1 1/2 hour would be best.
4. While the goat is cooking, drain the rice, which you should have left in cold water up until this point.
   Place in a different Dutch oven or pot and cover with a few inches of water.
   Bring to a boil. Boil for 8-10 minutes. Drain and set aside.
5. Fry the reserved onions in a small pan for an additional 10-15 minutes.
6. Once the meat is falling apart, season with salt and pepper and remove from heat.
7. Place half of the goat on the bottom of the large Dutch oven. Add half of the onions. Add half the rice on top and smooth out. Repeat with the remaining goat, onions, and rice.
8. Sprinkle with the rose water and the saffron milk. Top with cilantro.
   Cover with lid until ready to bake.
9. Preheat oven to 350°F (180°C).
   A half hour or hour before serving, roll out the chapati dough and use it to completely seal the top of the Dutch oven.
   Bake for 20 minutes.

spice mixture:

2 star anise

2 1/2 tablespoons coriander seed

1 teaspoon fennel seed

1/2 teaspoon cardamom

1 1/2 tablespoon cumin seed

3 teaspoons peppercorns

10 ground cloves

2 inch (5 cm) cinnamon stick, crushed

curry:

5 large onions, thinly sliced

2 inches (5 cm) ginger, minced

10 cloves garlic, minced

2 1/2 pounds (1200 g) goat, 1 inch (2.5 cm) cube

1/2 teaspoons ground turmeric

1/2 - 1 teaspoons chili powder

4 tablespoons yogurt

4 tablespoons tomato paste

biryani:

2 3/4 cups (550 g) basmati rice, triple rinsed, soaked in water

2 teaspoons rose water

pinch saffron in 1/2 cup (120 mL) hot milk

large handful cilantro, chopped

3/4 cup (180 mL) chapati dough, p. 45

Dal Makhani

serves 8-12 alone or 16-18 as part of meal

Lentils and beans end up on my menus a lot. Such inexpensive ingredients but ones that create a rich and powerful flavor. Dal seems to be a name that refers to a wide range of lentils, beans, and peas and may be the quintessential ingredient in Indian cuisine due to its availability, frugality, and amazing flavor. Make sure you don't forget to mix this regularly!

2 pounds (900 g) black mapte beans, rinsed three times

12 tablespoons unsalted butter

4 onions thinly sliced

4 inches (10 cm) ginger, minced

salt and pepper

20 cloves garlic, minced

6 ounces (175 mL) tomato paste

1-2 teaspoons chili powder

2 cups (480 mL) milk

1 cup (240 mL) cream

1. Place drained beans into a deep Dutch oven. Boil for 45 minutes, discard scum.

2. Fry onions in half the butter, 15 minutes.
Add garlic and ginger, 5 minutes.
Add tomato paste, chili powder, and salt and pepper. Stir and remove from heat.

3. Remove most of water from cooked beans, only leave enough to barely cover.
Add onions and milk and cream. Bring to boil.
Lower heat and simmer for at least 90 minutes, stirring every 5 minutes or so.
Add remaining butter and adjust seasoning.

Naan

makes 24 breads

The humble naan, brushed with some butter with a sprinkle of fresh cilantro, always wins my heart. It might seem excessive to have two breads for two courses, but I didn't hear anyone complaining! I doubled the recipe here, but it might be easier to handle one half at a time.

naan:

8 cups (960 g) all purpose flour

1/2 cup (120 mL) yogurt

5 teaspoons active dry yeast

4 teaspoons sugar

3 teaspoons salt

2 teaspoons baking powder

2 cups (280 mL) milk, hot, but
   not boiled

olive oil

garnish:

melted butter

fresh cilantro

1. Mix all ingredients less the milk on counter. Slowly add milk and knead into dough.
2. Knead for five minutes. Rub oil all over it. Place in bowl, cover and let double in size.
3. Divide into 24 balls. Roll out on floured surface.
4. Put dry frying pan on medium. Heat for 30 seconds until brown, flip and repeat. Brush with butter and sprinkle cilantro.

Gulab Jamun

serves 16-20

For over a decade, I have loved "Indian syrup balls," those amazing little balls found at the end of every Indian buffet. It took me going to an Indian market last year to figure out what they were called. This was a challenging recipe, but I am glad I made it. There are many recipes out there, but you have to trust your instinct with how much yogurt to add in. Also be aware that the balls will expand by at least 50% when fried. A friend judges Indian restaurants by their Gulab Jamun, and ours were the best he tried in years. Best Indian Restaurant is what I heard!

1. For the sauce, mix water, sugar, and cardamom. Boil until it turns slightly sticky, somewhere between half and half and maple syrup.
   Add rose water, set aside, keep hot.
2. Mix the flour, milk powder, and soda. Add oil. Stir milk and 4 tablespoons yogurt together and slowly add to flour. Add more yogurt, 1 tablespoons at a time, until a golf sized ball holds together. Bring dough into a ball, greasing hands if needed.
   Make 60 balls, they should be solid and not soggy.
3. Heat up a tall pot with oil to fry. Make sure your syrup is still hot. Carefully drop balls into oil in batches. Make sure they don't stick to the bottom. Heat until the balls turn dark brown, add to the syrup.
   Rest for three hours. Serve with the pistachios.

gulab jamun:

4 cups (600 g) milk powder
1 1/2 cup (180 g) flour
4 tablespoons vegetable oil, extra for greasing
4 tablespoons milk
8+ tablespoons yogurt
1 tablespoon baking soda
peanut oil for deep frying

syrup:

8 cups (1.6 kg) sugar
9 cups (2.2 L) water
1 1/2 teaspoon ground cardamom
3 tablespoons rose water

garnish:

1/2 cup (65 g) chopped pistachios

Mango Lassi

serves 12-18

6 - 7 large mangoes, pureed
1 1/2 teaspoon ground cardamom
6 cups (1.5 L) yogurt
sugar to taste

1. Perhaps the simplest recipe in the book. Blend all that stuff together, add as much sugar as you enjoy. Refrigerate at least an hour before serving.

Macao

I first heard about Macao through learning about the dish Fat Rice. The complexity of this dish was thrilling, and I was curious to see how the mixture of meats and fishes would work with all of these varied spices. The Portuguese occupied Macao for a long time, bringing with them the flavors of the West and every other territory they conquered. These flavors and techniques mixed with local Asian flavors and a unique mixture was born. After hours of Googling, I came across Abraham Conlon and Adrienne Lo's book entitled "The Adventures of Fat Rice". I owe them a debt of gratitude for the techniques and inspiration.

Guests: 10

The Game Plan

2-3 days before:

prep and freeze Croquettes (2 days)

prep Plum Sauce

marinate Pork and Chicken

make Batatada and Raspberry Sauce

day before:

4 pm   cook Pork

           cook Italian Sausage

4:30 pm   bake Chicken

5 pm   cook Chili Shrimp

           cook Garlic Mussels

day of:

2 pm   start Fat Rice

4 pm   prep greens and mushrooms

5 pm   cook Stir Fry

5:30 pm   assemble Fat Rice

6 pm   fry Eggplant

6:15 pm   fry Croquettes

Sweet and Sour Fried Eggplant in Sambal

serves 8-10

We are deep frying eggplant here. Lets be real, it is not a healthy dish, but it does not feel heavy or oily. The combination of oil and vinegar and the spicy Sambal that is added on top makes for a lovely combination. The dish is traditionally served with a Sambal Tumis, but I was running low on time so I cheated and used some jarred Harrissa sauce to serve.

1. Combine vinegar, sugar, ginger, bay leaves, lime juice, turmeric, tamarind, and water in a medium pot. Season with salt and pepper and bring to boil.
    Remove from heat and set aside.
2. Heat peanut oil in high pot. Deep-fry eggplant in small batches until golden and soft. It will look like cardboard as it soaks. About 45 seconds to a minute.
    Remove from oil and put it in the vinegar mixture.
    Soak for 20 minutes, drain, and arrange on a serving platter.
3. Serve with the sambal or harrissa.
    Sambal is more culturally appropriate, but I hate using that much dried chili, your call!
    Drizzle with the sambal or harrissa.
    Sprinkle the sesame seeds, green onions, and peanuts.
    Serve warm or cool.

sweet and sour eggplant:

3/4 cup (180 mL) rice vinegar

1/2 cup (100 g) sugar

1 inch (2.5 cm) ginger, minced

2 bay leaves

1 teaspoon lime juice

1/2 teaspoon turmeric

2 tablespoons tamarind paste

1 1/2 cup (360 mL) water

salt and pepper

peanut oil, for deep frying

2 pounds (900 g) Chinese
    eggplant cut into pyramids

garnish:

Sambal Tumis or Harissa to serve

sesame seeds, toasted

green onions, thinly sliced

roasted peanuts

Minced Meat Potato Croquettes

serves 8-10

This is another one of those dishes that requires a series of steps and is a bit labor intensive but incredibly worth it when you put it on the table. I prepared this recipe to serve around 15 guests, but only 10 were able to come. I thought I would have leftovers for days, but every single croquette was eaten that night! You will not regret making this dish. I used preserved mustard greens, but any preserved green would work!

filling:

1. Combine first 13 ingredients, chill overnight.
2. The next day, heat oil in a large saucepan. Add the bay leaf, stir, 1 minute. Add onion, 5 minutes. Add shallot and garlic, 2 minutes.
3. Add meat and cook, break up into little pieces as you cook. Cook until browned and thickened, 10 minutes. Add potato starch slurry and cook until thickened.

dough:

4. Boil potatoes, 20 minutes. Drain, rest, 5 minutes. Peel and mash and add potato starch. Cool.
5. Take a large piece of plastic, at least 22 inches (56 cm) long and place on counter. Spread 1/4 of dough at the bottom center of the plastic into a 4x12 inch (10x30 cm) strip. Fold the top of the plastic over and roll out to a 6x16 inch (15x33 cm) rectangle. Unfold plastic and trim. Add 3/4 inch (2 cm) filling along the bottom of the potato. Roll carefully like a giant sushi with help of the plastic. Seal up with plastic wrap and place in the freezer for one hour. Repeat with the rest of dough. make 4 logs.
6. Remove from plastic and chop into 1 inch (2.5 cm) pieces. Spread the potato to seal the filling completely. Defrost a bit if needed.
7. Toss each in flour, beaten egg, then bread crumbs. Freeze overnight.
8. Deep-fry for 4-5 minutes until deep brown and cooked through.

Black Bean Plum Sauce

1. Heat oil in small heavy pan. Add peppercorns, 2 minutes. Add onion, 5 minutes. Add garlic and ginger, 1 minute.
2. Add plums, sugar, vinegar. Cover and cook 15-20 minutes, stir occasionally.
3. Let cool and blend. Add water to thin if necessary. Season with salt and pepper.

filling:

1/4 teaspoon baking soda
1/4 teaspoon rice vinegar
1 1/2 teaspoon soy sauce
1 teaspoon Worcestershire sauce
1 tablespoon preserved greens
1/4 teaspoon brown sugar
pinch cinnamon
1/4 teaspoon curry powder
1/4 teaspoon chili powder
1/4 pound (115 g) ground pork
1/4 pound (115 g) ground beef
1 tablespoon olive oil
1 bay leaf
1/4 onion, chopped
1/2 shallot, minced
1 clove garlic, minced
salt and pepper
1 teaspoon potato starch in
  2 teaspoons cold water

dough:

4 pounds (1.8 kg) potatoes
10 tablespoons potato starch
2 teaspoons salt

breading:

1 cup (120 g) all purpose flour
3 eggs with 1 tablespoon water
1 cup (90 g) bread crumbs

finish:

peanut oil, to deep fry and salt

plum sauce:

4 tablespoons peanut oil
2 tablespoons fermented bean
1 tablespoons peppercorns
1 small onion, finely diced
6 cloves garlic, minced
1 inch (2.5 cm) ginger, minced
12 plums pitted
2 tablespoons sugar
4 tablespoons rice vinegar
salt and pepper

Fat Rice

serves 12-14

There is no denying it, this dish has many steps. The following five recipes are all parts of this dish. You could use a large shallow bowl to serve, but the dish fits perfectly into a 7 quart oval Dutch oven. Feel free to invent with the preparation of the separate parts, as long as the flavors are in the same family they should work well. This truly is a strange blend of flavors coming together into something resembling a paella. Perhaps this dish, in itself, is sufficient for the whole dinner.

1. Boil 1/2 cup (120 mL) vinegar, raisins, and 1 cup (120 mL) water, set aside.
2. Heat 3 tablespoons duck fat in a pan and toss the baguette cubes until they become crispy croutons. Season with salt and pepper.
3. In a large pot, cook the duck confit with 10 cups (2.5 L) water, scallions, ginger and 1 tablespoon salt. Bring to a boil, lower heat, simmer 1 hour. Reserve the duck meat, chop into small pieces once cooled. Reserve broth. Discard bones, ginger and scallions.
4. Heat oil in a Dutch oven. Add onion and bell pepper. Season heavily with salt. Cover and cook for 20 minutes on low heat. Stir to prevent burning. Uncover. Cook 15 minutes.
5. Add tomato paste, garlic and paprika. Cook an additional 30 minutes at lowest heat. De-glaze with remaining sherry vinegar. Season with salt and pepper.
6. Boil broth from the duck with the rice for 4 minutes only. Drain and discard the broth. Spread rice out on a large cookie sheet. Let it cool for 30 minutes.
7. Transfer rice to a large bowl. Drain raisins and add them. Add the chopped duck and the bell pepper onion mixture.
8. Preheat oven to 400°F (205°C).

continued on next page

1 cup (150 g) golden raisins

1/2 cup (120 mL) sherry or red wine vinegar + 2 tablespoons

4 inch (10 cm) piece baguette cut into 1/3 inch (1 cm) croutons

4 tablespoons duck fat

2 tablespoons olive oil

1 large onion, thinly sliced

1 large or 2 medium bell pepper, thinly sliced

4 cloves garlic, minced

1 tablespoons tomato paste

1/2 teaspoons paprika

2 duck confit legs

4 scallions, 1 inch (2.5 cm) pieces

4 inches (10 cm) ginger, thinly sliced

3 cups (600 g) jasmine rice

1 teaspoon chicken stock concentrate

1/2 cup (120 mL) water

to serve:

Glazed Pork p. 69

Turmeric Chicken p. 71

Chili Shrimp p. 71

Garlic Mussels or Clams p. 71

1 pound (450 g) Italian Sausage, grilled

1 cup (130 g) olives, Manzanilla

3 lemons, quartered lengthwise

4 eggs, quartered lengthwise

3 scallions, 1/2 inch (1.25 cm) slice

chili powder

9. Grease Dutch oven with 1 tablespoon duck fat. Add in the rice. Make sure to flatten surface. Make a canal along the center of it all the way across, 1 inch (2.5 cm) wide and 2 inch (5 cm) deep. Cook on medium/high for about five minutes. You are making a crispy crust. Mix the stock concentrate and water and add to the canal.
    Cover and cook for five more minutes.
    Place in the oven and bake for 30 minutes.
10. Reduce the heat to 300°F (150°C).
    If the chicken, pork, and sausage is cold, put on sheet and reheat for 10 minutes.
11. Arrange the meats, fish and croutons on the surface of the rice. If preparing ahead of time leave the seafood in the fridge for later. Reheat in oven if necessary before serving.
12. To serve, add the mussels/clams and shrimp, eggs, olives, lemons, and scallions.
    Pour the sauce from the shrimp over dish.
    Sprinkle chili powder over lemon and eggs.

Glazed Pork

1. Combine all ingredients save for cornstarch and pork in a small saucepan. Add a few tablespoons of water and simmer.
    Mix cornstarch with water before adding it into the sauce. Whisk and cook until thickened. Let cool.
2. In a bowl or plastic bag, combine half the sauce and the pork shoulder. Smear until pork is covered. Refrigerate overnight.
    Refrigerate remaining sauce.
3. Leave on counter until it reaches room temperature. Grill or broil for 8-10 minutes, flipping halfway through.
    Internal temperature should be 145°F (65°C). This is a good opportunity to also grill or broil your Italian sausage.
4. Slice into 1/2x3 inch (1x7.5 cm) pieces and baste with the remaining sauce.

2 1/2 tablespoons soy sauce
1/2 tablespoon black bean
  paste
1 teaspoon paprika
1/2 teaspoon cinnamon
1/2 cup (120 mL) dry white wine
1/3 cup (80 mL) honey
1 1/2 tablespoons corn starch
2 tablespoons cold water
1 pound (450 g) pork shoulder

Turmeric Chicken

1. Place ginger, scallions, 1/2 cup (120 mL) wine, curry, turmeric, vinegar, and chicken in large bowl. Mix, refrigerate overnight.
2. Heat oven to 400°F (205°C). Spread chicken on baking sheet and bake 30 minutes.
   Turn over once and baste regularly with the marinade remaining in the bowl.
3. Cook the remaining marinade with the remaining 1/4 cup (60 mL) rice wine.
   Mix corn starch with a few tablespoons cold water. Add into sauce.
4. Baste chicken with sauce before serving.

1 inch (2.5 cm) ginger, sliced thinly
3-4 scallions
   sliced in 1 inch (2.5 cm) pieces
3/4 cup (280 mL) rice wine,
   separated
1 teaspoon curry madras
2 teaspoons turmeric
2 teaspoons sherry vinegar
2 pounds (900 g) chicken wings
   separated at the joints
1 1/2 tablespoon cornstarch

Chili Shrimp

1. Combine bean paste, chili flakes, garlic, and shrimp. Mix well.
   Shell and de-vein the shrimp.
2. Heat oil in large skillet or Dutch oven.
   Add shrimp. Cook 1 minute on each side.
   Add wine, cover, cook 4-5 minutes.
3. Reserve sauce to serve over fat rice.

2 tablespoons fermented bean
   paste
1 tablespoon chili flakes
2 cloves garlic, minced
1 pound (450 g) large shrimp
2 tablespoons olive oil
1/2 cup (120 mL) dry white wine

Garlic Mussels or Clams

1. Heat oil in saucepan. Add garlic and chili flakes. Cook 1-2 minutes.
   Add remaining ingredients.
2. Cover and cook until mussels open. Season with salt and pepper.
   You may not need all of these for the rice, top pasta with the rest the next day!

2 tablespoons olive oil
4 cloves minced garlic
2 tablespoons chili flakes
zest of one lemon
2 teaspoons lemon juice
2 teaspoons sherry vinegar
1 cup (120 mL) dry white wine
2 pounds (900 g) mussel or clam
salt and pepper

Greens Stir Fried with Mushrooms and Papaya

serves 8-10

1 cup (240 mL) chicken stock

1/4 cup (60 mL) gin

1 tablespoon soy sauce

1 teaspoon rice vinegar

1/2 teaspoon sugar

salt and pepper

1 teaspoon potato starch in 1
   tablespoon cold water

1/2 green papaya, peeled and
   thinly sliced

6 tablespoons peanut oil

15 cloves garlic, minced

1 1/2 pound (675 g) various
   mushrooms, chopped

6 tablespoons preserved
   mustard greens

20 cups (1 kg) various greens

Vegetable dishes from Macao are few and far between. This dish seems more pan-Asian, but the flavors used paired very well with the Fat Rice dish. Be careful with the sauce here. I set the gin on fire and had to wait for five minutes until the fire subsided.

1. Combine first 5 ingredients in pan, boil. Stir in starch slurry, simmer to thicken a bit. Taste and season with salt and pepper.

2. Heat oil in a Dutch oven. Add garlic, 1 minute. Add all mushrooms, preserved mustard greens, and papaya. Cook 5 minutes. Add leaves, mix around to wilt the leaves. Add sauce to slightly reduce. Season with salt and pepper. Serve immediately.

Sweet Potato Batatada with Raspberry Sauce

serves 12-14

Such an amazing and simple dessert. It can be presented as is, but I wanted to elevate it with a red berry sauce. Simply take some fresh berries and cook for 10 minutes with a bit of lemon and as much sugar as you like.

1. Preheat oven to 375°F (190°C). Line large pan with some butter and 2 tablespoons sugar.
2. Combine coconut milk and powder. Separately, mix flour, baking powder, salt and coriander.
3. Whip egg whites until firm peaks form. Cream butter and sugar together. Add egg yolks one at a time. Add flour mixture. Add sweet potato and the coconut mixture. Very carefully, fold in egg whites.
4. Pour into pan and bake for 75 minutes or so. Cool. Dust with confectioners sugar.

2 pounds (900 g) sweet potato
   boiled and pureed
32 tablespoons unsalted butter
2 cups (400 g) sugar + 2 tablespoons
5 cups (450 g) coconut powder
2/3 cup (160 mL) coconut milk
1 1/2 cup (180 g) cake flour
1 1/2 teaspoon salt
2 tablespoons ground coriander
12 eggs. separated
confectioners sugar

sauce:
2 cups (100 g) red berries
1/2 cup (100 g) or so sugar
juice of 1/2 lemon

Thanksgiving

Thanksgiving is not a Russian holiday, but we have made the most of it. With work and travel, it is one of those rare holidays where all of us manage to be in the same place. We have adopted the American tradition of feasting on this day, but have made our own traditions. Over the years, I have invited international friends to my parents' home since they can rarely afford a ticket back home for a four day weekend. This year, Nico and I had the honor of inviting my family and all of our international friends to celebrate at our home. I continue to refuse to make turkey, which always felt like a sad, dry, giant chicken to me. Our tradition is roast lamb with herbs and lemon. Delicious every time!

Guests: 9

first course:

Smoked Salmon, Horseradish, and Dill Crostini		79
Sardèle in Saòr Crostini		79

main course:

Herb and Lemon Crusted Roast Lamb		82
Roast Acorn Squash with Fresh Figs		83
Mushroom and Shallot Tarte Tatin		85
Bouillabaisse	France	149
Salad with Lemon Caper Dressing	Housewarming	171

desserts:

Smetannik		87
Blueberry Pie		91
Cannelés Bordelais	France	155

The Game Plan

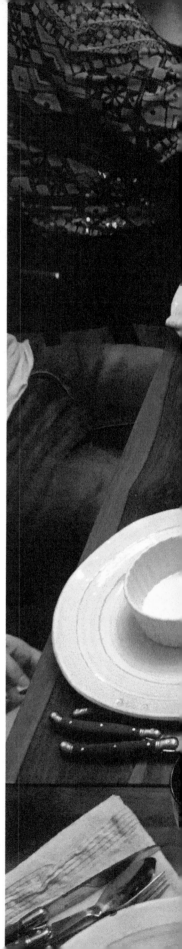

2-3 days before:

prepare Sardèle in Saòr topping

day before:

bake Focaccia or Baguettes

make Smetannik

assemble Blueberry Pie

make batter for Cannelés Bordelais

make herb paste and marinate Lamb

day of:

10 am	bake Blueberry Pie
11 am	bake Cannelés Bordelais
11:30 am	make Tarte Tatin
12:30 pm	make Acorn Squash
1:30 pm	make Bouillabaisse and Rouille
2:30 pm	put Lamb in oven
5 pm	assemble Crostini
5:30 pm	make Salad

Crostini Two Ways

serves 10-12

Salmon, horseradish and herbs. That flavor keeps creeping into my dishes of late. Try it on butter seared salmon as well! My trip to Venice inspired me to start our evening with this pair of crostini. I figured I would still be cooking when people arrived and we can have an informal first course of "hand food" and wine. This is a very simple fresh pairing that does not take too much effort to combine. It is well worth the minimal effort you will need to put into it. It can be served on a variety of breads, I have used Focaccia (p. 109) and Baguette (p. 145). Definitely have fresh bread as the vehicle for your flavors.

1. Mix together first four ingredients for sauce.
2. Toast bread, smear sauce.
   Top with salmon and dill.

Salmon, Horseradish, and Dill Crostini

1 cup (240 mL) crème fraîche, strained yogurt, or sour cream
2 tablespoons Dijon mustard
3 tablespoons horseradish
pinch of sugar, salt/pepper
8 ounces (225 g) smoked salmon
dill springs

Gonzo and I argued about this dish a bit when I first introduced it during the Venetian dinner. Sweet and vinegary, "they won't go for it", he said. I was almost convinced to take out the raisins, but I am glad I kept them. Sardines are amazing! I don't know why everyone here is so afraid of sardines and anchovies. Dusted with flour and fried, they turn decadent, especially when paired with the vinegar flavor of the marinated onions and the sweetness of the raisins. Make this dish several days in advance, it gets better with time. And don't be afraid if you have too much liquid, the sardines soak up a lot.

1. Season flour with salt and pepper, coat sardines. Brown in oil, set aside.
2. Preheat oven to 350°F (180°C).
   Toast pine nuts, 5 minutes.
3. Cook onion in olive oil for 20-30 minutes. Add vinegar. Add pine nuts and raisins.
4. Layer onion mixture and sardines. Leave in fridge to absorb for at least a day.

Sardèle in Saòr Crostini

1 pound (450 g) small sardines
flour to coat
salt and pepper
olive oil
4 ounces (115 g) pine nuts
4 large onions, thinly sliced
12 ounces (360 mL) white vinegar
1/2 cup (45 g) white raisins, soaked in hot water and drained

Herb and Lemon Crusted Roast Lamb

serves 8-10

1 head garlic, peeled

4 lemons, juiced, zest peeled off
   in strips

1 bunch sage, stems discarded

1 bunch rosemary, stems
   discarded

1/2 bunch parsley

1/2 cup (120 mL) olive oil

salt and pepper

bone in lamb, 5-6 pounds
   (2.2-2.7 kg)

This is one of the oldest recipes in this book. I have made a version of this lamb for Thanksgiving and any other holiday when someone would buy me a lamb leg since I was in high school. It was inspired by my father. When we had a bit of money for meat in Belarus in the summer, we would take our lamb into the woods, start a fire and stab it all over and shove garlic in before baking it. My dad would walk around in the woods and find an evergreen tree with little berries, I think it was juniper. We would place that with the meat over the fire and allow it to roast. I wanted to incorporate the garlic and smoked herb flavor and add in some freshness by adding lemon juice and zest. Please do not overcook the lamb!

1. Place zest and juice of lemon with the remaining ingredients in the blender to make a rough paste.
    Adjust ingredients as needed to get a workable consistency.

2. Allow meat to rest at room temperature for an hour. Place in a Dutch oven.
    Stab the meat all over and smear with the paste. Refrigerate for at least four hours, but preferably overnight. Bring to room temperature before roasting.

3. Preheat oven to 425°F (220°C).

4. Bake 20 minutes.
    Lower heat to 325°F (165°C).
    Bake approximately 20 minutes per pound of lamb roast, or until the inside temperature reaches 135°F (57°C).
    Allow meat to rest 10 minutes, it will rise to 145°F (63°C).

Roast Acorn Squash with Fresh Figs

serves 8-10

I needed a vegetable for this dinner, and I saw a recipe that incorporated sweet potato and fig. I figured the sweetness of the sweet potato could be replaced with the equally sweet acorn squash. I happened to have some on hand. Acorn squash is annoying to cut into wedges, but the dish is worth the effort, just don't chop off your finger as you go.

2-3 acorn squash
  sliced along crevices
4 tablespoons balsamic vinegar
2 tablespoons sugar
12 green onions, 1 1/2 inch
  pieces
6 tablespoons olive oil
1 red chili, thinly sliced
8 ripe figs, quartered
6-8 ounces (170-225 g) goat
  cheese

1. Preheat oven to 425°F (220°C).
    Toss squash in 4 tablespoons olive oil and salt and pepper.
    Arrange on a baking sheet and bake for 25 minutes.
    Allow to cool.
2. Place balsamic and sugar in small pan.
    Simmer until thickened, 2-4 minutes.
3. Heat remaining oil and cook green onions and chili, 2-3 minutes.
4. Arrange squash on platter.
    Top with figs, onions and drizzle with balsamic vinegar.
    Top with goat cheese, if you like.
    I serve it both ways.

Mushroom Shallot Tarte Tatin

serves 8-10

Apple Tarte Tatin is traditional. I made a Peach Tarte Tatin for our French dinner (p. 157), to shake it up. Here, I decided to use the puff pastry again but go for a more savory approach. I love porcini mushrooms and have dried ones on hand at all times. If you use dried porcini, make sure you reserve the water that you rehydrate them in. That makes an amazing mushroom stock, or can add flavor to anything that would otherwise call for water. Here the mushrooms are paired with sautéed shallots and the sweetness of balsamic vinegar. You can serve it warm or cold, but the puff pastry is a bit flakier when it its warm.

2 tablespoons pine nuts

6 large shallots, peeled and
  halved lengthwise

2 teaspoons olive oil

1/4 cup (60 mL) balsamic
  vinegar

1 teaspoon sugar

3 tablespoons unsalted
  butter, divided

1 pack frozen puff pastry
  1 pound (450 g)

8 ounces (225 g) mushrooms,
  torn to bite sized pieces
  preferably porcini

1 garlic clove, minced

3 ounces (85 g) chèvre or
  burrata

1/2 cup (10 g) arugula

1/2 ounce (15 g) Parmesan

to serve:

olive oil

lemon juice

1. Preheat oven to 400°F (205°C). Toast pine nuts for 4 minutes. Set aside.
2. Toss shallots in oil, season with salt and pepper. Bake for 20-25 minutes.
   Remove leathery outer layers.
3. Bring vinegar and sugar to simmer in a small pan, stir until syrupy.
   Stir in 1 tablespoons butter, remove from heat.
4. Arrange shallots cut side up in an oven proof skillet. Attach two sheets of defrosted pastry and roll them out a bit to even out. Lay pastry out on top of the shallots in the skillet and fold in the edges to make a crust. Prick with fork. Bake 25-30 minutes until golden.
5. In a medium skillet, heat 2 tablespoons butter and cook mushrooms and garlic, stirring often, for 5-8 minutes. Season with salt and pepper.
6. Let tart set until cooled. Carefully invert onto a plate. Top with mushrooms, chèvre, Parmesan, arugula, and pine nuts.
   Drizzle with oil and lemon juice and serve.

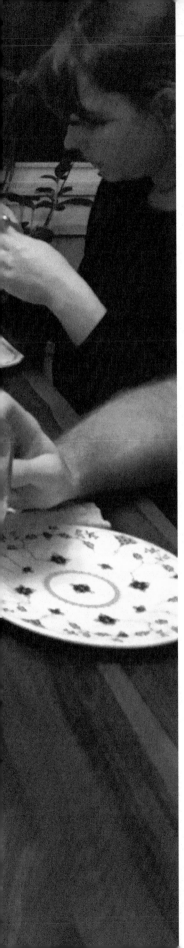

Smetannik

serves 8-10

This is one of the things that made me fat after we came to America. I have always loved this cake and, after we found it in Russian stores both in North Carolina and Maryland, I continued to eat it like a maniac. In Belarus, I had to walk and take the bus wherever I went, but living in suburbia, I couldn't work those buttery sour cream calories off anymore. I don't blame Smetannik. It is one of the most amazing cakes in the world and I will keep eating it. Make sure you split the cake into as many thin slices as you can so the sour cream and buttercream can soak in.

continued next page

cake:

5 eggs

2 cups sugar

2 cups sour cream

2 cups flour

1 1/2 teaspoon baking soda

1/2 teaspoon salt

1 teaspoon white vinegar

3 tablespoons cocoa

1/2 cup (100 g) apricots
finely chopped

1 cup (125 g) crushed
walnuts

sour cream filling:

4 1/2 cups (1 L) sour cream

2 1/4 cups (450 g) sugar

3 teaspoons vanilla

3 tablespoons amaretto

buttercream:

36 tablespoons unsalted
butter

1 cup (200 g)
+ 3 tablespoons sugar

6 egg yolks

1 1/2 cup (360 mL) milk

3 tablespoons vanilla

chocolate ganache:

3/4 cup (130 g) dark
chocolate

1 tablespoon unsalted
butter

cake:

1. Preheat oven to 350°F (180°C).
   Boil water. Soak apricots for 10 minutes.
2. In a bowl, mix together flour, salt, and baking soda.
   In a stand mixer, blend together eggs and sugar.
   Carefully add sour cream.
   Add the flour mixture slowly.
   Add the vinegar.
3. Separate dough into two batches.
   Add cocoa and crushed walnuts to one half of dough.
   Add drained apricots to the second half.
4. Pour into two buttered cake pans, use release pans if you
   have them.
   Bake for 20-25 minutes until toothpick comes out clean.
   Cool cakes completely.
5. Carefully slice each cake into 3-4 thin layers, as thin as
   you can make it.

buttercream:

6. In saucepan, mix egg yolks, milk, and sugar on low heat
   to boil.
   Simmer 2 minutes and cool completely.
7. Beat butter with vanilla until fluffy.
   Add cooled egg mixture and continue beating.
   Place 1/3rd in pastry bag and reserve remaining for filling.

sour cream filling:

8. Mix all ingredients.

assembly:

9. Add one layer to bottom of spring-form pan.
   Add 1/2 cup (120 mL) sour cream mixture, and a bit of
   buttercream.
   Repeat for all cake layers.
   Add only sour cream mixture to top of cake.
10. Refrigerate for at least 4 hours.
    Remove from spring-form, place on platter.
11. Combine chocolate and butter in saucepan, melt.
    Place in plastic bag, cut a slit, and create pattern on top
    of cake.
12. Pipe the reserved buttercream around the sides of the
    cake.

Blueberry Pie

serves 6-9

For the desserts, I figured I would create something from each of the cultures that was present that evening. We are a Russian family, so the previous pages feature a Smetannik. Our guests are all French, so I brought back Cannelés Bordelais (p. 155). We came together to celebrate an American holiday, so for one dish, I decided to cave in to tradition and include my blueberry pie. Use the finest milled pastry dough you can find for the crust and add as little water as possible for the flakiest results.

crusts:

24 tablespoons unsalted
   butter

4 cups (480 g) cake flour

8-12 tablespoons cold
   water

2 teaspoons salt

filling:

5 cups (500 g) blueberries

1 cup (200 g) sugar

1 teaspoon lemon juice

1/2 cup (60 g) flour

2 tablespoons unsalted
   butter

1/2 teaspoon cinnamon

assembly:

1 egg, lightly beaten

sugar

1. Mix softened butter and flour together, by hand. Always make crusts by hand, a mixer will overwork your dough.
   Add salt and a bit of water to bring it together into a ball.
   Add as little water as possible, and mix as little as possible. Pieces of butter in the dough is OK.
   Divide into two balls. Cover in plastic.
   Refrigerate for 30 minutes.
2. Roll out one crust to fill your pie dish. It helps to roll on top of a sheet of plastic and then transfer into your dish with its help.
   Roll out second sheet and slice into 3/4 inch (2 cm) strips.
3. In a small pot, mix together blueberries, sugar, lemon juice, flour, butter, and cinnamon.
   Add a bit of salt. Cook until warmed through.
3. Pour into crust. Basket weave a top crust. Pinch edges with fork.
3. Preheat oven to 400°F (205°C).
   Brush with egg mixture and bake for 30-40 minutes, until set.

South of the Border

I wanted to be together with friends for the 2016 Presidential election night. The results seemed so sure at the time, but we were also all a bit nervous. We figured why not gather together and celebrate what America has always been about, immigration and the melding of cultures. Specifically, we decided to celebrate the shared culinary traditions on the Mexican border. We featured dishes popular in Mexico and New Mexico and featured the shared flavors and ideas that flow through the border in between. Most of the recipes for this dinner were Gonzo's creation, and he kindly shared them on our website. In the following pages, I will share with you the recipes that I created for the dinner and list what else was included so you can find them on ChezNousDinners.com.

Guests: 8

The Game Plan

2-3 days before:

make Queso Fresco, drain

make Sour Cream

day of:

12 pm	prepare Carnitas
2 pm	make Refried Beans
3 pm	make dough for Churros
5:30 pm	assemble and bake Enchiladas
6 pm	make Salad
	fry Churros and melt chocolate before
	dessert

Enchiladas Verdes de Carnitas

serves 12-14

I insisted on carnitas for this dinner. I was originally only supposed to be in charge of dessert. Roasting the meat with orange was a revelation. It turned out incredibly delicious and could be used in a variety of different recipes or eaten on its own. The Verde sauce is made with tomatillos, which I thought would be so difficult to find, but it seems they are everywhere and cost less than tomatoes.

carnitas:

1. Combine all ingredients in Dutch oven. Cover and transfer to oven at 300°F (150°C) for 2 hours.
2. Remove pork and orange halves. Blend and reduce the braising liquid over high heat until thick.
3. Pull meat into small chunks, toss in the glaze, and spread onto a slotted rack over a cookie sheet. Broil until brown and crisp.

salsa verde:

1. Blanch tomatillos. Drain, set aside.
2. Heat oil in saucepan. Add onion and cook 3 minutes.
   Add garlic and chili, 1 minute.
3. Put onion mixture and tomatillos in blender.
   Pour back in saucepan, simmer. Remove from heat add salt.
4. Place 4 tablespoons of carnitas at one end of warmed tortilla, roll and place on oven safe platter.
5. Preheat oven to 350°F (180°C). Cover rolled tortillas with sauce and cheese crumbles. Bake until cheese is melted and serve.

carnitas:

4 pounds (1.8 kg) pork roast
  1 inch (2.5 cm) cubes
2 cups (480 mL) water
1 onion, peeled, halved
2 tablespoons lime juice
1 teaspoon dried oregano
1 teaspoon ground cumin
2 bay leaves
1 orange, juiced and halves
  reserved

sauce:

1 1/2 pound (675 g) tomatillos
  quartered and cored
2 tablespoons olive oil
1/2 white onion
  coarsely chopped
2 cloves garlic, minced
cow horn pepper
  de-seeded, chopped
1 bunch cilantro, chopped
1 tablespoon salt, to taste

assembly:

12 corn tortillas
1 3/4 cup (400 g) queso
  fresco, p. 99

Queso Fresco

serves 6-10

1. Mix milk and salt in stock pot over medium heat.
   Heat slowly to 185°F (85°C), stirring constantly.
   Line strainer with cheesecloth.
2. Remove milk from heat, stir in circular motion and add vinegar.
   Allow milk to sit for a few minutes until it separates into curd and whey.
   Add extra vinegar if it does not happen.
3. Strain, reserve whey for baking or other recipes.
   When mostly strained, gather the cheesecloth at its edges and tie together and hang off of faucet to drain for 2 hours.

I am a big fan of cheese and have been trying to explore the creation of fresh cheeses this year. The recipes for all are similar but use different acids, which all give the curds a slightly different flavor. Queso Fresco can be made with either apple cider vinegar or lime juice, but lime juice queso tends to be a little more delicate.

1 gallon (3.8 L) whole milk

6 tablespoons salt

4-6 tablespoons cider vinegar

Crema Mexicana

serves 6-10

This version of sour cream was delicious. We used it as a side for a lot of the dishes that Gonzo made for the meal. It lasts for at least a week, so if you use sour cream regularly make a big batch. This is a richer cream, close to crème fraîche, thus the deliciousness!

1 cup (240 mL) heavy cream

4 tablespoons buttermilk

1. Sterilize a glass container. Microwave with water or place in the oven for a bit. Cool the container. Add heavy cream and buttermilk. Swirl together.
2. Cover with plastic wrap. Leave on counter at room temperature for 12-18 hours. The cream should have thickened, if not, add a bit more buttermilk and repeat.
3. Refrigerate, it will get thicker as it ages.

Refried Beans

serves 6-10

1 pound (450 g) dried beans
   pinto or black

1 1/2 large onion, chopped

2 cloves garlic, minced

1 tablespoon olive oil

large handful parsley, chopped

1/2 teaspoon chili flakes

salt and pepper

1/4 cup (60 mL) olive or
   vegetable oil

1. Cover beans in water, rinse. Cover again and soak overnight.
2. Drain and rinse a couple more times. Place in Dutch oven and cover with a few inches of water. No salt! Bring to a boil. Reduce to simmer, skim surface regularly. Once all foam is gone, maybe 10 minutes, add 1 onion and garlic. Simmer for at least an hour and a half. Add water if needed.
3. Salt to taste once soft and add vegetable oil, some parsley, and dried chili flakes. Continue to simmer until thick.
4. In a separate Dutch oven, heat up oil and add the 1/2 onion. Cook for 5 minutes. Add half the beans, mashing them as you put them in. Stir. Add remaining beans and continue mashing and stirring until a thick paste is formed. I like to leave some of the beans intact. Season with salt and pepper.

Salad with Cilantro Avocado Dressing

serves 6-10

I may not always include it here, but almost all of my meals incorporate a salad of some sort. I always have a dish or two that I consider "the impressive ones," and inevitably those dishes are full of fat, or cheese, or starch. I need the zest and bite of a vinegary salad to break up the heavy flavors of those dishes. So in the end, it is the humble salads that help the stars shine.

2 avocados
  bite sized slices, divided
2 limes, zested and juiced
3 cloves garlic
1/2 bunch cilantro
1/4 cup (60 mL) olive oil
10 radishes, thinly sliced
1 cup (165 g) yellow corn,
  blanched
10-12 cups (200-250 g) arugula
salt and pepper

1. In a blender or mixer, combine garlic, zest and juice of limes, cilantro, olive oil, and 1/2 of one of the avocados.
Blend until combined. Add more lime or oil to make thinner if needed.
Season with salt and pepper.

2. Assemble salad when ready to serve. Toss all of the ingredients together and season with more salt and pepper necessary.

Churros with Chocolate Sauce

serves 6-10

I had churros in Spain, but they are also incredibly popular in Mexico. After an argument over their origin, we did some digging and could not come up with a clear answer. It appears that they might have even come from China by way of Portuguese colonials. Either way, the churro is a popular dish in Mexico and I was glad I made them for our dinner. The dough is really hard to pipe if you don't have a churro pipe. I just gave up and rolled little sausages. They taste just fine either way.

churros:

2 cups (480 mL) water

5 tablespoons sugar

1 teaspoon salt

4 tablespoons olive oil

2 cups (240 g) all purpose flour

2 quarts (2 L) vegetable oil for frying

1/2 cup (100 g) sugar

1 teaspoon cinnamon

chocolate sauce:

2 bars dark chocolate

3 tablespoons butter

paprika, to taste

1. In a saucepan, mix water, sugar, salt, and olive oil.
   Bring to a boil and remove from heat.
2. Stir in flour.
   Roll into sausage shapes, or alternatively put through churro press. The dough is very thick, it will not go through a pastry bag.
3. Heat oil and fry in small batches until golden.
4. Remove from oil onto a paper towel lined plate.
5. Coat in sugar cinnamon mixture.
   Arrange on serving platter.
6. Melt chocolate with butter, mix in spice and serve in a small container.

Venice

This past spring I went back to Italy and visited Venice for the first time. It was beautiful! I wanted everything! The food, the art, the shoes, the hand blown glassware! Nico couldn't join me so I tried to bring some of it home with me. You could call this an Italian dinner since I pulled some recipes like Osso Buco from less coastal areas. To honor the waters that will someday sink Venice, I used sardines and anchovies heavily. Those are staples in Italian dishes and sneak their way in to add excitement to many sauces. I finally got to make a huge batch of Tiramisu. I once saw Gordon Ramsey yell at someone for how bad theirs was. This inspired me to try it out myself. Gonzo came by and made some homemade pasta since I just purchased a pasta cutter. I am really fond of this menu, maybe I will pull a repeat someday!

Guests: 13

The Game Plan

2-3 days before:

make Sardèle in Saòr topping
make Pesto
make Mozzarella

day before:

make Focaccia
prepare Tiramisu
prepare sauce for Bignoli in Salsa

day of:

11 am	start Osso Buco, cook on back burner
12 am	make Saffron Risotto, keep warm
1 pm	make Saffron Pears and Whipped Cream
2 pm	prepare Bignoli dough, wait to cut
6 pm	make Panzanella
6:15 pm	cut Bignoli pasta, cook just before serving
6:30 pm	prepare and assemble Crostini
	add extra cocoa to Tiramisu to serve

Focaccia

serves 12-14

1. Mix yeast and water.
   Add half of bread flour.
2. Leave covered to rise until it starts to fall again, about an hour.
3. Knead in remaining flour and salt.
4. Transfer to a clean, oiled bowl. Cover.
   Let rise for at least 1 hour.
   Knock it back.
5. Oil hands and spread dough on oiled, parchment lined cookie sheet.
   Smear with olive oil and let rise 1/3rd of volume.
6. Preheat oven to 400°F (205°C) with convection fan on, or 425°F (215°C) without.
   Press fingers into dough, push in rosemary sprigs and spread with fleur de sel.
7. Bake until golden, about 45 minutes.

When I lived in New York, I would love going to Eataly to order the two things I could afford: a slice of focaccia topped with sausage and peppers, and a tiny cup of gelato. The texture of the bread was to die for. I think it was the airiness and the oil. I still feel like mine is not quite the same, but it holds the toppings of a crostini much better. Do not be stingy with the olive oil.

---

4 teaspoons active
   dry yeast
2 3/4 cups (660 mL) warm
   water
8 cups (960 g) bread flour
2 teaspoons salt
olive oil
finishing salt
rosemary sprigs

Fresh Mozzarella and Pesto Crostini

serves 12-14

I've been on a quest to make my own mozzarella, and this dinner party was the perfect occasion to perfect it. Melting the cheese and getting it into a proper ball was the tough part for me. Don't be disappointed if it does not work perfectly the first time. It will still taste good. Call it deconstructed burrata and scoff at complaints. I paired it with a homemade basil and zesty arugula pesto. I find it to be a very successful combination. Buy the best ingredients that you can afford for the pesto and adjust to your taste.

pesto:

1. Grind up all ingredients, season with salt and pepper, adjust to taste.
2. Slice up focaccia, brush with olive oil and broil for a minute or so until crispy and gold.
3. Add one teaspoon of pesto to crostini, top with slice of fresh mozzarella.

fresh mozzarella:

1. Stir water and citric acid together.
2. Pour milk into Dutch oven and add the citric acid mixture.
   Warm to 90°F (32°C), stirring frequently.
3. Remove from heat, add rennet and stir for 30 seconds.
   Stop stirring, cover and leave for 5 minutes.
4. Milk should be set into curds. Cut them into 1 inch squares.
   Heat milk to 105°F (40°C) stirring slowly. Add salt. Leave for another 5 minutes. Drain the curds.
5. Microwave for 30 seconds. Squeeze out all whey you can. Repeat twice.
6. Knead on counter to shape a ball. Keep in water until you serve.

pesto:

1 head garlic

3 cups (75 g) basil leaves

2 cups (40 g) arugula

1/3 cup (45 g) pine nuts

1/2 cup (100 g) Parmesan

1/2 cup (120 mL) olive oil

salt and pepper

fresh mozzarella:

1 gallon (3.8 L) milk

1 cup (240 mL) water

1 1/2 teaspoon citric acid

1/4 teaspoon liquid rennet

6 tablespoons salt

crostini:

20 small slices focaccia

olive oil

Bignoli in Salsa

serves 12-14

salsa:

1. Heat olive oil in Dutch oven or high rimmed pan.
   Cook onions in oil for 20-30 minutes.
2. Add anchovies and wine.
   Cook until anchovies fall apart, around 5-10 minutes.
   Add butter. Season with salt and pepper.
3. Fold into pasta, reserving a bit to garnish on top.

bignoli noodles:

1. Beat eggs and milk, incorporate into flour pile on counter.
2. Mix until ball forms.
   Knead 5 minutes on a floured surface.
   Form into tennis-sized balls.
   Cover and rest 1 hour.
3. Dust machine with flour and run through machine at thickest setting.
   Fold like a letter, and roll through again.
   Repeat 2-3 times until smooth.
   Trim and cover with towel, repeat for remainder of dough balls.
4. Run through the cutting roller on the small slicer.
   Dust with flour to keep separate.
5. Boil salted water. Cook 2-3 minutes.

Bignoli is traditionally a round whole wheat pasta, which is exclusively eaten with anchovy salsa. The sauce is a revelation. Venice made me fall in love with all mixtures of onions, small salty fishes, and wines. This is a subtle and delicious sauce which is very easy to make. Pasta making is incredibly therapeutic, like edible Play-Doh.

———

salsa:

6 medium onions, thinly sliced

3 tablespoons olive oil

40 anchovies with oil

2 cups (480 mL) of white wine

2 tablespoons unsalted butter

salt and pepper

bignoli noodles:

1 1/2 cup (180 g) whole wheat flour

2 1/2 cups (300 g) all purpose flour

4 eggs

1/2 cup (120 mL) warm milk with 2 tablespoons butter

Osso Buco with Saffron Risotto

serves 12-14

This is a very rich pairing, so you do not need to have large portions. It is, however, very delicious! Saffron has earned its renown; just a pinch elevates the flavors in the rice. Osso Buco means bone hole in Italian. When I was young, I remember my mom was always keen on eating the tail bone of the chicken and the marrow of bones. We thought she was crazy. I wish I knew what the big deal was back then!

saffron risotto:

1. Add oil and half the butter to a Dutch oven. Add onion and cook until transparent, about 15 minutes.
2. Add rice, stir 2 minutes. Add vermouth and 2 cups (500 ml) broth. Add saffron. Stir regularly until liquid is absorbed.
3. Add one cup broth at a time, stirring.
4. Once all absorbed, add Parmesan and remaining butter.

osso buco:

1. Preheat oven to 350°F (180°C). Heat half of oil in a Dutch oven. Season shanks with salt/pepper. Coat in flour. Brown on flat sides. Set aside.
2. Add remaining oil and onion to Dutch oven. Add carrots, celery, garlic, and spices. Season with salt and pepper, sauté for 10 minutes.
3. When it starts sticking, add the wine and cook for 2 minutes. Add tomatoes and 1 cup (250 ml) water. Season with salt and pepper. Add meat back to pot. Cover.
4. Place in oven and roast for 2 hours. Check after an hour.
5. Serve with Saffron Risotto.

saffron risotto:

1 onion, finely chopped

6-7 cups (1 1/2 - 1 2/3 L) chicken stock

1 3/4 cup (350 g) Arborio rice

1 cup (240 mL) dry vermouth

3 tablespoons unsalted butter

pinch saffron

grated Parmesan

osso buco:

4 tablespoons olive oil

6 pieces bone in shank (1 1/2 inch or 4 cm thick)

1/2 cup (60 g) flour

3 carrots, finely chopped

3 celery stalks, finely chopped

1 large onion, finely chopped

2 cups (480 mL) white wine

2 sprigs rosemary, leaves chopped

4 sprigs thyme, leaves

2 garlic cloves, minced

28 ounce (825 mL) tin diced tomatoes

salt and pepper

Panzanella

serves 8-10

Panzanella is one of my favorite ways to use up old bread! At it's core, it is very similar to a salad we ate in Belarus. The Russian version involves a couple of tomatoes and cucumbers with some salt and pepper drenched in sour cream and eaten with a crust of bread to soak up the delicious mixture of tomato and sour cream. The Italian version replaces the sour cream with a vinaigrette. I generally add the burrata to retain some of that creamy texture, but since the rest of this meal is already so rich, I omitted it for this dinner.

1. Cover the sliced shallot in vinegar. Season with salt and pepper. Allow to marinate for at least 10 minutes to get rid of the bite.
2. Preheat oven to 450°F (230°C).
   Tear up the bread and place in a bowl with the garlic and some oil. Toss to coat.
   Spread on baking sheet and bake for about 10 minutes until crispy and golden.
3. Finish the salad about 20 minutes before serving. Otherwise, it will be too dry or too soggy.
   Combine tomato, cucumber, radish, garlic toast, and shallot mixture (reserving half of vinegar) in a large bowl.
   Add burrata if using.
   Drizzle olive oil to taste and mix around.
   Season with salt and pepper and adjust seasonings. Add more vinegar if needed.

1 large shallot, thinly sliced

2 tablespoons red wine vinegar

4 ounces (115 g) of old bread, ciabatta or baguette (about 4 inch/10 cm piece of baguette)

2 cloves garlic, minced

2 ripe tomatoes, cored and chopped into wedges

1 large or 3 small cucumbers, peeled, halved and chopped into half circles

5 radishes, thinly sliced

4 sprigs fresh basil leaves

olive oil

salt and pepper

optional for a fuller meal:
   8 ounces (225 gram) burrata or fresh mozzarella, ripped into pieces

Tiramisu

serves 12-14

1. Combine coffee, rum, and 1/2 cup (100 g) sugar in a large bowl.
   Mix until sugar is dissolved. It helps if the coffee is a bit warm.
2. In a stand mixer, whisk egg whites until firm.
3. Separately, add remaining sugar and Marsala to egg yolks.
   Whisk until pale and fluffy.
   Add mascarpone.
   Carefully fold in egg whites.
4. Dip lady fingers in coffee mixture until wet but not falling apart.
   There is only a second or so between a bit too crunchy and soggy mess, so don't get distracted.
5. Make layer of about 12 lady fingers in a large flat serving dish.
   I used a 14 inch (35 cm) shallow bowl. Cover with half of mascarpone mixture.
   Add cocoa, sprinkle through a sieve.
   Repeat step 5 with rest of ingredients.
6. Refrigerate for at least 4 hours. When ready to serve, dust another layer of cocoa on top.

Everyone loves Tiramisu! I have never met anyone who doesn't. Adults love the sophisticated mixture of cream and coffee. Kids love their first opportunity to consume some booze. What can go wrong? Tiramisu is not hard to make, you don't even need to bake. However, I strongly discourage using white sponge cake or pre-made "Tiramisu filling" that is sold in grocery stores. That is not Tiramisu, that is closer to a trifle.

———

3 cups (720 mL) coffee

8 tablespoons rum

1 1/4 cup (250 g) sugar

6 eggs, separated

1/2 cup (120 mL) Marsala

18 ounces (500 g)
  mascapone

24 lady fingers

cocoa powder

Saffron Poached Pears with Marscapone Whipped Cream

serves 12-14

I love visiting farmer's markets on the weekends. One morning, I was roaming the stalls and found someone selling "ugly" bosc pears, a giant basket for $3. I had to buy it. I didn't manage to eat that many of them by the time the Venetian dinner came about. As more and more guests responded, I figured I might need a second dessert. I thought I would use the pears. I had marscapone left over from the Tiramisu and sent Nico to the store for some whipped cream. I had one glass of white wine left from the rest of the recipes and figured a bit more of "saffron yellow" on our dinner table couldn't hurt. Thus this dish was born. It is a very lovely, light dessert.

8-10 bosc pears, peeled and quartered

1 cup (240 mL) white wine

6 cups (1 1/2 L) water

1 cup (200 g) + 1/4 cup (50 g) sugar, separated

pinch saffron

16 ounces (475 mL) whipped cream

6 ounces (170 g) mascarpone

1 teaspoon vanilla

1. Combine wine, water, 1 cup (200 g) sugar, saffron and pears in a saucepan.
   Cook on low heat for about an hour.
2. Remove pears from pot and let them cool.
3. Increase heat and reduce syrup to a thick sauce.
   This may take up to an hour longer.
4. Whip cream until soft peaks form.
   Fold in mascarpone, 1/4 cup (50 g) sugar, and vanilla.
5. Serve pears with syrup and topped with cream.

Perú

My best friend is from Perú and he keeps telling me about the delicious food and restaurants in Lima. On a trip to San Francisco we went to La Mar, an amazing Perúvian restaurant and I fell in love. When we lived together and Rafael's parents would visit, I would get to try Causas and other dishes embedded with key limes, cilantro, and the heavenly aji amarillo! I miss living with Rafael. He came to visit me in Baltimore around our birthday, yes our birthdays are a week apart! We decided to throw ourselves a dinner party and make Perúvian food. Rafael was in charge of the stew and causa, and I was in charge of the sugary dishes and odds and ends. We have a good time as a team! I hope you enjoy these dishes.

Guests: 9

The Game Plan

If you are working alone, you might want to make the Seco de Carne and the potato mix for the Causa the day before. The Causa should be assembled the day of and the Seco de Carne is easily reheated. You can prepare the Taqueños in advance, fry the day of.

day of:

10 am	prepare Suspiro de Limeña
12 pm	make Alfajores
1 pm	prepare meat for Seco de Carne
	make Frijoles Guisados
2 pm	assemble Taqueños
2:30 pm	make Avocado sauce
3 pm	make Causas
5 pm	make Seco de Carne
6 pm	make Rice
	fry Taqueños

Taqueños

serves 8-10

It seems like every culture has some version of a cheese stick. Maybe cheese is what will brings us all together in the end. Maybe I will write a cheese treaty! This is a simple and delicious dish. The lime flavored avocado sauce pairs really well with the deep fried pastries. Make sure you seal the wrappers carefully to avoid the cheese from seeping out.

taqueños:

1. Cut mozzarella into 20 matchstick shapes.
2. Wrap each piece in a wonton wrapper, like you would a burrito.
3. Heat up oil and deep fry the taqueños until they are golden and puffy.

avocado sauce:

1. Mash avocado.
2. Mix all ingredients together and season with salt and pepper to taste.

taqueños:

20 wonton wrappers
16 ounces (450 g) fresh
   mozzarella cheese
oil for deep frying, peanut oil
   works well

avocado sauce:

1 avocado
1 tablespoon olive oil
1 teaspoon key lime juice
salt and pepper

Causa

serves 8-10

1. Peel and chop potatoes and boil for 20 minutes until soft.
   Mash to a fine texture.
2. Mix aji amarillo paste, juice of 8 key limes, and potatoes.
   Season with salt and pepper.
3. Add some lime juice to sliced avocados.
4. Mix some mayonnaise into the crab. Season with salt and pepper.
5. If you want to expose the layers, line the interior of a spring-form pan in plastic wrap. Oil plastic.
   Alternatively, use a serving dish.
6. Alternate layers of potato mixture with layers of avocado, tomato, crab and shrimp.
   Reserve some shrimp or avocado for decoration.
7. Chill to set. If serving on a platter, carefully slide knife around edges. Invert onto serving platter. Open spring-form, and remove plastic wrap.
   Decorate the top with reserved shrimp or avocado.

Causa is hard to describe. It seems odd but it is an amazing dish. I first had it at Rafael's parent's Christmas party. Yellow potato mash flavored with aji amarillo and key lime was layered with avocado, tomato, tuna, and shrimp. I could never remember the name so I didn't figure out how to make it until rather recently. Since we were making ours in Baltimore, we used crab instead of tuna.

———

2 pounds (900 g) yellow potatoes
1/2 cup (120 mL) olive oil
16 ounces (450 g) crab
juice of 10 key limes
4 tablespoons aji amarillo paste
2 avocados, sliced
1 cup (240 mL) mayonnaise
12 shrimp, cooked, peeled
3 tomatoes, sliced

Seco de Carne

serves 8-10

When we were in high school, Rafael taught me that in Peruvian cooking you never have just one one starch. Each meal is incomplete without the presence of both potatoes and rice. This rich stew gets its flavor from the aji amarillo paste, beer, and a seemingly excessive amount of cilantro. We have eaten many versions of this stew in our time living together. It is hearty,delicious, so make it anytime!

seco de carne:

1. In a large bowl, combine beer, paprika, aji amarillo, and beef. Marinate overnight.
2. In a large Dutch oven, heat oil and brown the beef. Set aside. In the same pan, sauté onion and garlic for five minutes. Quickly brown meat. Reserve beer broth. Add remaining vegetables.
   Add stock and beer broth, bring to simmer.
   Add all remaining ingredients.
3. Cover and simmer on low heat until tender, about 2 hours.
4. Serve with rice and beans.

rice:

1. Sauté garlic in oil in a sauce pan, 2 minutes. Add rice and mix. Add salt and water. Boil. Lower heat and simmer, 15 minutes.
2. Sauté peas in some butter. Mix into the rice.

seco de carne:

4-5 pounds (2-2.5 kg) beef, neck or other cut, cubed
2 cups (480 mL) corn beer, or regular beer
1 teaspoon paprika
3 tablespoons aji amarillo paste
1 teaspoon oregano
1/2 cup (120 mL) vegetable or olive oil
1 red onion, finely chopped
4 cloves garlic, minced
1 cup (240 mL) cilantro puree (3 bunches of cilantro and 1/2 cup/120 mL water)
4 cups (960 mL) beef stock
3 large carrots, cut into thin rounds
12 ounces (340 g) corn kernels
12 ounces (340 g) peas
2 pounds (900 g) potatoes
salt and pepper

rice:

4 cups (800 g) jasmine rice
1/4 cup (60 mL) olive oil
3 cloves garlic, minced
8 cups (scant 2 L) water
2 tablespoons butter
3 cups (450 g) peas
salt and pepper

Frijoles Guisados

serves 8-10

Perhaps the third indispensable side dish in a Peruvian meal is the frijol. The yellow canary bean is used most, but I could not find any for the life of me. I visited three grocery stores. In this recipe, I used dried kidney beans instead. There are some flavor similarities between this dish and the first few steps of the refried beans from the last chapter, but here the beans remain intact in a thinner sauce and the aji amarillo paste creates a distinct flavor that pairs with the other dishes in this meal. What you will notice in this chapter is that the garlic and onion are sautéed at the same time. The French/ Italian tradition calls for the onion to be sautéed for 10 minutes with garlic introduced for 1 minute at the end to avoid burning. Here they are sautéed for five minutes together.

one pound (450 g) dried kidney
   beans, or yellow canary beans
1/4 cup (60 mL) olive oil
   or vegetable oil
1 large red onion, chopped
4 cloves garlic, minced
1/4 cup (50 mL) aji amarillo
   paste
salt and pepper

1. Rinse the beans and remove any pebbles. Soak in water overnight.
2. Heat oil in a large Dutch oven and sauté onion and garlic for about 5 minutes.
3. Add aji amarillo paste, mix to combine. Sauté for 3 minutes.
4. Drain beans.
    Add to the pot and mix thoroughly to combine.
    Cover with a couple of inches of water.
    Bring to a boil. Lower to simmer and cook for about one hour until beans are soft.
    Season with salt and pepper.

Alfajores

serves 8-10

In high school, when Rafael's parents would come back and visit, his mom would always bring some gift from Perú. I developed a collection of alpaca hats, scarves, and wraps, but my favorite things were the alfajores that would come in small paper packages. The little cookies were hardly larger than a nickel and coated in confectioner's sugar. The rich filling was otherworldly. For some reason, I never thought that one could make their own. I just associated them with the tiny boxes that arrived from Perú. The filling is one ingredient! Sweetened condensed milk boiled in its container in a large pot of water. It has to boil for at least four hours so make sure that the water does not boil off, otherwise the can might explode. Keep adding water.

alfajores:

2 1/4 cups (270 g) cake flour

1/2 cup (120 g) unsalted butter, softened

3 1/2 tablespoons confectioners sugar

filling:

1 can sweetened condensed milk

1. Place sweetened condensed milk, intact and in sealed container into a tall pot filled with water, 8-10 inches above top of can. Boil for about four hours.
2. While the condensed milk is cooking, preheat oven to 375°F (190°C).
3. Combine the softened butter with the cake flour and sugar. Mix until the dough is even. Roll into a ball, cover, chill for a half hour.
4. Roll out on floured surface until about 1/6 inch (4 mm) thick.
   Cut into circles or other shape.
5. Place onto parchment lined cookie sheet. Bake for 12 minutes, or until barely golden.
6. Wait to cool completely.
   Add some mixture to the middle of a cookie and top with a second.
   Arrange on platter and spread confectioners sugar to serve.

Suspiro de Limeña

serves 8-10

caramel pudding:

1. Combine the two milks in a heavy bottomed pan and simmer over low heat, stirring continuously until the mixture thickens. About 1 hour.
Your arm will hurt.
2. Take off the heat.
Whisk in beaten egg yolks.
Leave to cool and then pour into shallow dessert vessels.

Port merengue:

1. Combine sugar and Port in a small pan and boil until syrupy. Again, mix regularly. Maybe the other arm?
The syrup should form a continual thread when pulled up with a spoon, at least a half an hour.
2. Beat egg whites until they form soft peaks.
Continue beating while carefully adding the hot syrup.
3. Pipe the meringue on top of the caramel and dust lightly with cinnamon.

I wanted to try this dish simply because of how labor intensive it was. This was hard to make! But it is so decadent! I was really proud of how this dish came together. The name means the "Sigh of Lima." If that doesn't inspire you to want to try it I don't know what will. You can make a large dish and serve it to the whole table or in single serve vessels.

———

caramel pudding:

1 14 1/2 ounce (430 mL)
   can evaporated milk
1 14 ounce (415 mL) can of
   sweet condensed milk
8 egg yolks

Port meringue topping:

1 cup (240 mL) Port
1 1/2 cup (200 g)
   granulated sugar
4 egg whites
ground cinnamon

France

Like my Russian forefathers, I have been obsessed with French food and culture for as long as I can remember. This chapter feels the most like home and represents the recipes that I have been refining for the longest time. Since living in Baltimore and dating Nicolas, our group of French friends has been exponentially expanding. In the beginning it was just Nico and Corentin. These days, the French make up more than half of any dinner party. Coming back from a summer abroad, Nico and I wanted to bring our friends together for dinner. I figured French would be a great way to start.

Guests: 9

The Game Plan

day before:

prepare batter for Cannelés Bordelais

prepare batter for Madeleines

prepare dough and onion for Pissaladière

day of:

10 am	start Baguettes
	make two crusts for Quiche and Tarte, refrigerate
10:30 am	place Baguette dough in oven to rise, 45 minutes
	make Rouille
11 am	prepare fillings for Quiche and Tarte
11:30 am	second rise Baguettes, 1 hour
	Bouillabaisse
12:30 pm	shape Baguettes, final rise, 1 hour
	bake Quiche and Tarte
1:30 pm	bake Baguettes
2 pm	bake Madeleines
2:30 pm	bake Cannelés Bordelais
3:30 pm	make Pêche Tarte Tatin
5 pm	assemble and bake Pissaladière
6 pm	remove cheese from fridge and bring to temperature

Baguettes

makes 3 loaves

1. Mix water and yeast, leave for 10 minutes.
2. Mix flour into yeast water. Leave to hydrate for 20 minutes.
3. Add salt and knead for 10 minutes.
4. Oil, cover, and leave to rise in cold oven with the pilot light on to double in size. About 45 minutes.
5. Remove onto counter. Spread into 10x10 inch (25x25 cm) square and fold as depicted in the images, next page. Fold the sides into the middle, flip 90 degrees fold into the center again.
5. Place seam-side down back into bowl. Cover, let rise for another hour in the cold oven.
6. Take a clean kitchen towel and spread with flour. Fold into long waves with crevices for 3 loaves.
7. Divide baguette into three sections. Spread dough into a long rectangle about 6x9 inches (18x22 cm), page 147. Roll into a cigar shape and pinch the seam. You will have a 9 inch (22 cm) long cigar. Hold at the ends and stretch out like taffy until 12-15 inches (30-38 cm) long. Place in crevice on towel. Repeat.
8. Cover with another clean kitchen towel and allow to rise for another hour.
9. Place a metal pie pan or comparable dish into the oven on the low rack, reserving the top rack for baguettes. Preheat oven to 450°F (230°C) with the convection fan, or 25°F (15°C) higher without.
10. Spread corn meal or flour onto a large cookie sheet. Transfer baguettes carefully onto floured cookie sheet, try not to deflate them.
11. Cut 1/4 inch (6 mm) deep slits along baguettes with a razor blade. Place in oven. Place ice cubes into lower pan.
12. Bake for 30 minutes or until dark brown on the outside. Flip halfway if no convection.

Baguettes took me so long to master! I tried many different techniques and made at least 30 loaves of bread before they looked anything like a baguette from a French bakery. Eventually, I realized the importance of moisture in the oven with the loaves and started using ultra-sharp utility blades to score the bread. I have since then developed the best combination of the four simple ingredients. Buying a convection oven sealed the deal! Now this is my default loaf of bread.

———

1 1/2 cup (360 mL) warm water

1 teaspoon active dry yeast

3 1/4 cups (390 g) bread flour

1 1/2 teaspoon salt

oil for greasing dough

1/2-1 cup (200 mL) ice cubes

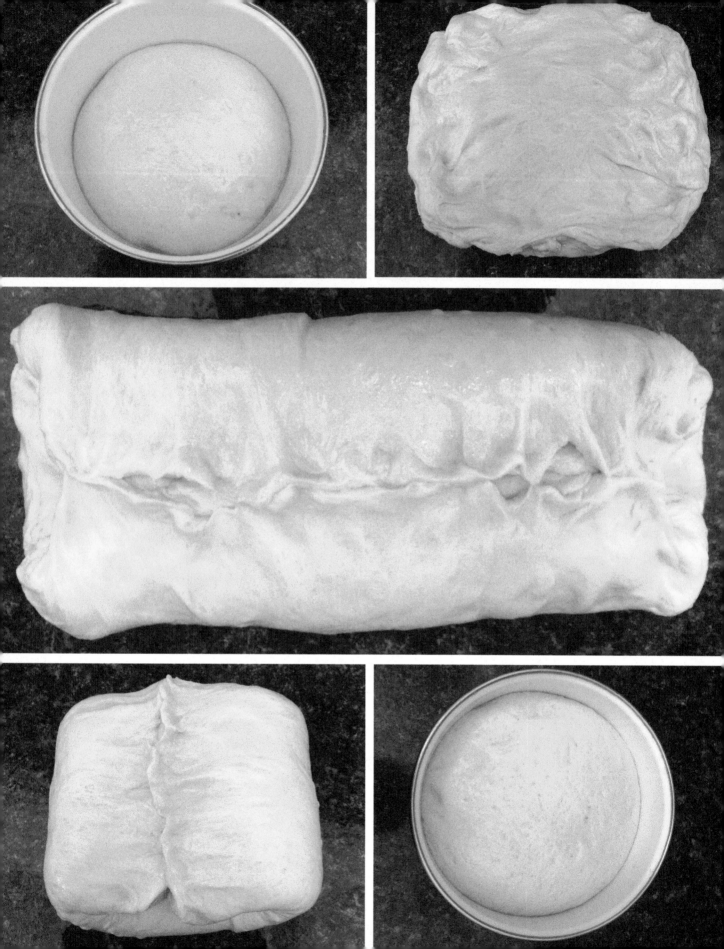

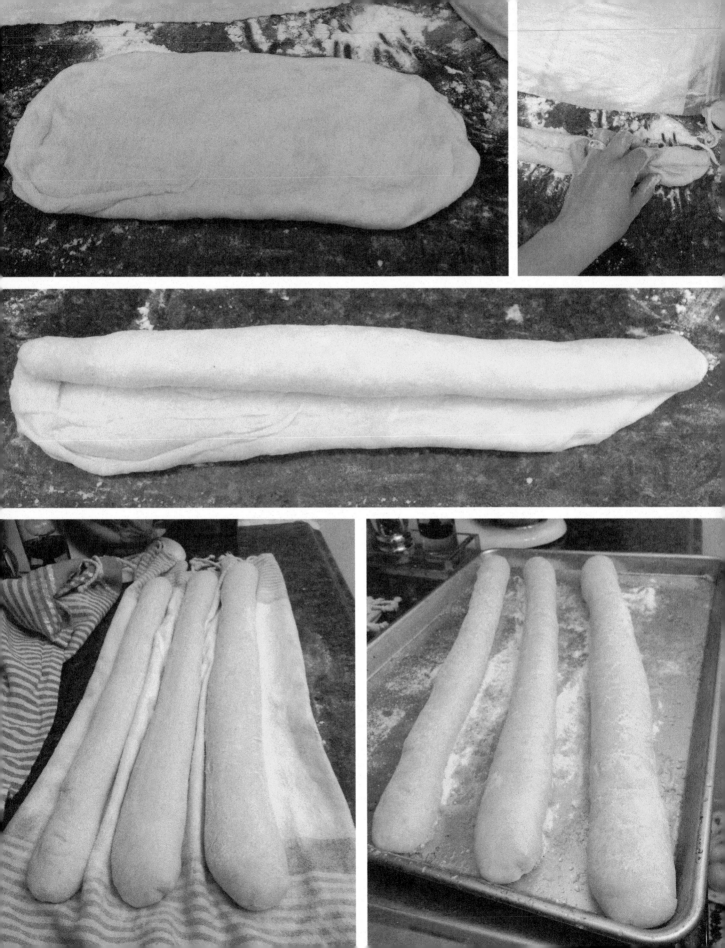

Bouillabaisse with Rouille

serves 12-14

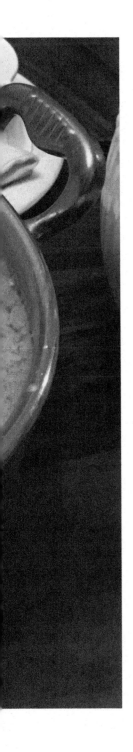

This dish is foolproof! Bouillabaisse originates from Marseilles and was made of cheap cuts of fish and eaten by fishermen who reserved the better cuts to sell. Since then, it has become a quintessential dish. It is served with baguette and a rouille drizzled into the soup to add flavor, much in the same way that sour cream is added to the Russian Borsht. Our friends Romain and Vanessa are from Marseilles and attended this dinner. They confirmed for us that it is just as it should be. Enjoy!

bouillabaisse:

1. Heat oil, add fennel, onion, garlic, parsnip, leek and fennel seed in a Dutch oven or large heavy bottomed pan. Cook for 10 minutes.
2. Combine one cup (240 ml) of stock and saffron in a small bowl. Steep 10 minutes.
3. Quarter, deseed, and chop tomatoes. Add tomato paste to veggies, 1 minute. Add tomatoes, bay leaves, thyme, and all stock. Season with salt and pepper cook 30 minutes.
4. Add cayenne, fish and prawns. Boil for five minutes. Add mussels. Cook until shells open, 3-5 minutes.

rouille:

1. Grind garlic, saffron, and cayenne. Add vinegar blend until smooth. Fold in remaining ingredients. Season with salt and pepper.

bouillabaisse:

2 bulbs fennel, thinly sliced, trimmings reserved

1 onion, finely chopped

2 parsnips, finely chopped

6 cloves garlic, finely chopped

2 leeks, white parts, sliced

6 tablespoons olive oil

1 teaspoon crushed fennel seeds

8 cups (scant 2 L) fish stock

2 pounds (900 g) tomatoes

2 tablespoons tomato paste

2 bay leaves

2 teaspoons fresh thyme

pinch cayenne

4 pounds (1.75 kg) cod, sea bass, or white fish, cubed

1 pound (450 g) shrimp

1 pound (450 g) mussels

pinch of saffron

salt and pepper

rouille:

2 cloves garlic, minced

1/4 teaspoon cayenne

1/2 pound (225 g) roast peppers, drained, diced

2 teaspoons red wine vinegar

1 cup (240 mL) mayonnaise

pinch of saffron

salt and pepper

Tarte au Chèvre et aux Courgettes

serves 6-8

1. Preheat oven to 350°F (180°C).
    Prepare crust, pierce bottom
    with fork a few times.
    Add some dry beans over a
    piece of parchment.
    Bake for 10 minutes.
2. In a large bowl, mash up the
    goat cheese and blend in eggs,
    basil, salt and pepper.
3. Remove crust from oven and
    save beans for another crust.
    Pour egg mixture into crust.
    Slice zucchini thinly.
    Arrange in a pattern on top of
    the egg mixture.
    Sprinkle with Gruyère and some
    more salt and pepper.
4. Bake for another 30 minutes until
    set and crust becomes a bit
    golden.
    Can be baked at the same time
    as the Quiche Lorraine.

*This is a great
combination for a
summer meal. I found
the the inspiration to
use goat cheese and
zucchini in the "Carnet
Retrouvé," a book
featuring recipes
found in a cooking
journal of a French
cook penned in 1870.
Nico's parents gave
us this book for
Christmas and I have
been teaching myself
more French by
translating the recipes.
I have learned a lot!*

———

1 pastry crust (p. 91)
  only make half recipe
2 small zucchini, thinly sliced
11 ounces (310 g) goat
  cheese
1 ounce (30 g) grated
  Gruyère
4 eggs
handful of fresh basil leaves
salt and pepper

Quiche Lorraine

serves 6-8

This is my favorite quiche. The combination of fluffy crust with leeks, bacon, and egg is wonderful. I generally think about quiche like an egg filled pizza. A variety of vegetables, cheeses, and meats can be mixed with egg to create wonderful results. The previous page featured the combination of goat cheese and zucchini, but you can also try kale and sun-dried tomato, or cauliflower, onion, and paprika. The options are endless.

1 pastry crust (p. 91)
   only make half recipe
2 leeks, thinly sliced
1 medium onion, diced
4 eggs
1/2 cup (120 ml) heavy cream
1 heaping cup (250 mL)
   sour cream
pinch nutmeg
6 ounces (170 g) bacon
3/4 cup (85 g) grated Swiss
   or Gruyère cheese
salt and pepper

1. Preheat oven to 350ºF (180ºC). Chop bacon and cook until crisp. Set aside.
2. Drain out most of oil.
    Use a bit of oil to sauté the leeks and onion, 30 minutes.
3. Mix eggs, cream, sour cream, nutmeg, and salt and pepper in separate bowl.
4. Spread leek mixture over one uncooked crust.
    Sprinkle bacon on top.
    Use fork to mix around a bit.
5. Sprinkle with cheese and cover with egg mixture.
6. Bake 25-35 minutes, can be baked at the same time as the Tarte aux Courgettes.

Cannelés Bordelais

makes 18-20 cannelés

I love desserts, always have. I love the complexity of flavor and nuance of mixing different fruits and flours together. Nico likes sweets too, but we seem to gravitate towards different flavors. I love a Sacher Torte for the intense blend of apricot syrup, dense chocolate cake, and ganache crust. Nico loves sugar cookies.

When we were in Versailles, we stopped into a bakery for a coffee and Nico bought me his favorite pastry, the Cannelé Bordelais. This is definitely not a sugar cookie! The dark crispy crust with a chewy rum flavored middle is wonderful, albeit somewhat tough to create. It is achieved by a very high milk to flour ratio, it will seem wrong, but trust the process.

1. Pour milk into a small saucepan. Add vanilla. Bring to boil. Cool.
2. Melt butter. Allow to cool.
3. Whisk eggs, egg yolks, and sugar.
4. Whisk and add in the following order: rum, melted butter, flour and finally vanilla milk. Cover and refrigerate overnight.
5. Melt beeswax and butter. Heat molds a bit. Pour wax mixture into molds and pour out to create a thin coat. Freeze for at least 10 minutes.
6. Preheat oven to 450°F (230°C). Fill molds 3/4 of the way up. Fill just before baking.
7. Bake f15 minutes. Lower heat to 375°F (190°C). Bake 45 minutes. The cannelés will try to slide up and out of their molds as they bake. Take them out of the oven for a minute to let them sink back in.
8. Eat the day they are made, they will not keep well.

2 teaspoons vanilla

2 cups and 2 tablespoons (300 mL) whole milk

3 1/2 tablespoons butter

2 eggs + 2 egg yolks

2 cups (250 g) confectioners sugar

1 1/2 tablespoon rum

1 cup less 2 tablespoons (110 gram) fine cake flour

molds:

1 ounce (60 g) beeswax

1 ounce (60 g) unsalted butter

Pêche Tarte Tatin

serves 12-14

1. In a large, oven-proof pan, cook sugar with water, without stirring, until it caramelizes.
2. Remove from heat and add butter to stop cooking. Allow to cool.
3. Place peach halves cut side up into sauce pan.
4. Preheat oven to 325°F (165°C).
   Bake for 1 1/2 hours.
5. Roll out the pastry dough and connect together to 1 inch (2.5 cm) wider than the pan. Cut a circle shape. Arrange on top of the peaches and tuck the edges in.
6. Preheat oven to 350°F (180°C).
   Bake for 35 minutes. Refrigerate for a minimum of two hours for the caramel to set.
7. Dip pan in hot water for 15 seconds to release from pan, invert onto serving dish.

Tarte Tatin is a French classic. It is generally prepared with apples, however, I had a basket full of large, fuzzy peaches from the market. I decided to try this variation. It turned out well. In the future, I might use slightly smaller peaches and reduce the recipe so the pastry will be a little easier to flip over. With the weight of the fruit, caramel, puff pastry, and the copper pan I was cooking it in, I almost dropped it on the floor!

---

tarte tatin:

7 large peaches
1/2 cup (120 mL) water
1 1/2 cup (300 g) granulated sugar
9 tablespoons unsalted butter
2 puff pastry sheets

Madeleines

serves 12-14

1. Mix zest, sugar, eggs, and honey. Whip until pale and fluffy.
   Fold in flour and baking powder. Melt butter. Add melted butter, mix to combine.
2. Refrigerate for 12 hours.
3. Preheat oven to 400°F (205°C). Butter and flour the molds. Refrigerate for 15 minutes. Fill molds 3/4 of the way up with batter and bake for 8-12 minutes.

madeleines:

zest of 2 lemons, or 1 lemon and
  one orange
rounded 3/4 cup (160 g) sugar
rounded 1 1/3 cup (170 g) cake flour
2 tablespoons baking powder
12 1/2 tablespoons unsalted
  butter
4 eggs
2 tablespoons honey

Pizza Housewarming

Nico and I moved into our new home in April 2016. It took some time to rebuild walls and make our kitchen, but once all of the plaster dust settled we wanted to invite all of our friends to our home. This dinner is not quite like the others. We did not really have courses, and it was not much of a sit down dinner since we had so many folks over. Any of the other dinners can be served in this format if you don't have a huge table or want to make use of an outdoor/indoor space on a summer afternoon.

Guests: 20

The Game Plan

day before:

prepare dough for pizzas, make 1/2 crust per person

prepare topping for Pissaladière

prepare Mozzarella if making your own (p. 111)

bake Blueberry Pie (p. 91)

bake and chill Cheesecake

bake and chill Key lime Pie

bake Baguettes or other bread to serve with salumi

day of:

11 am   make Marinara

chop up vegetables and ingredients for pizzas

1 pm   prepare Salad

bring cheeses up to room temperature

plate salumi and olives

2 pm   have two pizzas ready to go into the oven as guests arrive

bake more pizzas as guests arrive

Pizza Crust and Marinara Sauce

makes 2 crusts and 6 cups sauce

After making your own crust and sauce, you will never go back to frozen pizza and canned marinara. All canned sauces taste sugary in comparison. This is a great idea for a party that does not require too much work ahead of time and can be assembled quickly as guests arrive. You have all of the materials ready, spread some toppings on a piece of crust and bake. The crust also freezes really well. Make sure to bring it back up to room temperature before baking. The following recipe makes enough dough for two crusts.

pizza crust:

1. Combine all ingredients in mixer or by hand until ball forms.
2. Knead on floured counter for 5 minutes. Grease bowl, cover, and rest for 1 hour.
3. Divide and use.
   Bake prepared pizzas at 425°F (220°C) with convection on for 20 or so minutes, unless stated otherwise. If you are using an oven without a convection fan, bake at 450°F (235°C).

marinara sauce:

1. In a Dutch oven, heat olive oil.
   Sauté garlic for about 1 minute.
2. Mix in tomato paste and cook for 1-2 minutes until aromatic.
   Pour in tomatoes. Be careful, it likes to splatter at this point.
   Season with salt and pepper and add herbs. Simmer for about 20 minutes. Taste and adjust seasoning.

pizza crust:

4 cups (480 g) bread flour

1 teaspoon sugar

2 1/4 teaspoons active dry yeast

2 teaspoons salt

1 1/2 cup (360 mL) warm water

2 tablespoons olive oil

marinara sauce:

4 cloves garlic, minced

3 tablespoons olive oil

4 tablespoons tomato paste

2 28 ounce (785 mL) containers
   of crushed tomatoes

handful of fresh basil leaves,
   chopped

handful of fresh oregano,
   chopped

salt and pepper

Pissaladière

serves 6-10 each

The Pissaladière is my favorite pizza variation. Unlike many of the other dishes, this pie actually originates from Nice, in Southern France. This dish is featured as the first course in our French dinner. During this meal, we experimented a bit with the pizza. As you might note in the photograph, half of the pizza features a marinara while the other half is brushed with olive oil and garlic. Both sides are delicious. Serve the tomato-free version for the French dinner. The onion mixture in this recipe is enough for two pies.

1. Heat olive oil in a large pan.
   Add onions, sauté for 10 minutes.
   Add garlic and sauté for about 1 minute.
   Add capers, water, and thyme.
   Cook until glossy and almost falling apart, about 40 minutes.
2. Once ready to assemble, roll or toss crust to about a 12x16 inch (30x40 cm) rectangle.
   Preheat oven to 425°F (220°C) with convection fan on.
   Place on cookie sheet dusted with some flour or corn meal.
   Spread either garlic oil or marinara.
   Top with half of onion mixture.
   The recipe is enough for two pies.
   Top with mozzarella cheese.
   Arrange 12 anchovies and olives.
3. Bake for 20 minutes or so until the crust in the center is set and the edges are golden.

1 pizza crust
3 tablespoons olive oil
2 pounds (900 g) onion, thinly sliced
4 tablespoons capers
3 teaspoons thyme
1/4 cup (60 mL) water, more as needed
12 anchovies
1 cup (115 g) low moisture mozzarella, shredded
12 olives, I use Kalamata
salt and pepper

base:
2 tablespoons olive oil with minced garlic or marinara sauce

167

Each of these pizzas uses one half of the crust recipe on (p. 165) and calls for a base of either Marinara, (p. 165), or olive oil mixed into some garlic. Bake each pie at 425°F (220°C) for about 20 minutes unless stated otherwise. Add ingredients on top of crust in the order they are listed. Salt and pepper the top of each pie and drizzle with a bit of olive oil before baking.

Margherita

marinara, 1/2 cup (120 mL)
handful fresh basil leaves

8 ounces (225 g) fresh
mozzarella, sliced

Onion Ricotta

garlic and olive oil
1 medium onion, sliced,
  caramelized in some oil
1/2 cup (80 g) corn

6 tablespoons ricotta
handful fresh basil leaves,
  chopped, after baking

Bell Pepper Pizza

garlic and olive oil
5 bell peppers, thinly sliced
1 tablespoon fresh rosemary, chopped

8 ounces (225 g) fresh
mozzarella, torn to bits

Sausage, Red Onion, and Mushroom

garlic olive oil, with 1/3 cup
 (40 g) Parmesan
3 teaspoons rosemary, chopped

1/4 teaspoon red pepper
1 Italian sausage, casing removed
1/2 small red onion, thinly sliced

4 ounces (115 g) fresh mushrooms
cup (115 g) low moisture mozzarella
parsley, garnish after baking

Tuna and Capers Marinara

marinara, 1/2 cup (120 mL)
chopped thyme and rosemary

1/2 red bell pepper, thinly sliced
1 can tuna in oil, drained

cup (115 g) low moisture mozzarella
1 tablespoon capers

Asparagus, Fingerling Potato, and Chèvre

garlic olive oil
4 scallions, thinly sliced
cup (115 g) low moisture mozzarella

8 tablespoons chèvre, crumbled
8 ounces (225 g) asparagus,
 chopped, tossed in oil

1/3 - 1/2 cup (40-60 g) Parmesan
5 ounces (140 g) fingerling
 potatoes, boiled, sliced

Salad with Lemon Caper Dressing

serves 12-14

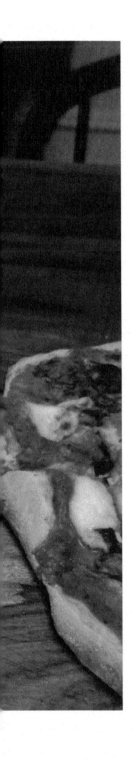

1. To trim the bottoms of asparagus, hold each piece at the head and tail, bring ends together to break at the natural breaking point.
Discard the bottom half.
Cut remaining stalks into 1 1/2 inch (4 cm) pieces.
Blanch for a 3 minutes and toss in iced water to stop cooking.
2. In a blender, combine capers, anchovies, lemon zest and juice, garlic, and olive oil.
Blend until combined.
Taste and season with salt and pepper. Adjust quantities of flavors if needed.
3. Assemble salad when ready to serve. Toss all of the ingredients together and season with more salt and pepper if necessary.

There is a lot of cheese going on in this meal. I wanted to add a light salad with some lemony tang. I incorporated flavors and ingredients that were already part of the pizzas to round out the meal but also to use up extra ingredients.

———

4 tablespoons capers

4 anchovies

2 lemons, zested and juiced

3 cloves garlic

1/4 cup (60 mL) olive oil

10 radishes, thinly sliced

1/2 bunch asparagus

10-12 cups (200 g) arugula

salt and pepper

Cheesecake

graham cracker crust

4 (8oz) packs of cream cheese
1 ¼ cup sugar
1 ½ cup sour cream/yogurt
2 tsp vanilla or 4 tbsp
5 large eggs   lemon ≈

topping 2 tbsp sugar + ½ cup
                 sour cream/yogurt

preheat oven to 475°
pan w/ 1½ in water

Cheesecake

serves 8-12

Nico loves cheesecake and raspberries. I generally make the recipe topped with some quickly cooked raspberries with some sugar and lemon juice. In this image, the cheesecake is served with pears that were sautéed in some butter with sugar and brandy. Really, you can use any variety of fruit, jam, or ganache.

1. Preheat oven to 450°F (230°C) with convection fan on.
   Prep a large pan with 1/2 - 3/4 inch (2 cm) water.
2. Mix first four ingredients to create graham cracker crust.
   Cover 9 inch (23 cm) spring-form pan in several layers of aluminum foil. Press graham cracker mixture into the bottom of the pan in an even layer.
3. Mix remaining ingredients in mixer. Pour on top of graham crackers. Place pan in water dish. Bake for 10 minutes.
3. Lower heat to 325°F (165°C). Bake for 50-60 minutes longer, or until the edges turn golden.
4. Spread with sour cream topping and refrigerate for at least four hours before removing from pan.
5. Serve alone or topped with any number of fruit toppings.

graham cracker crust:
1 1/2 cup (150 g) graham crackers, ground
1/3 cup (70 g) sugar
6 tablespoons unsalted butter, melted
pinch of salt

cheesecake:
4 8 ounce (225 g) packs of cream cheese
1 1/4 cup (250 g) of sugar
1/2 cup (120 mL) sour cream or yogurt
2 teaspoons vanilla or 4 teaspoons lemon juice
5 eggs

topping:
1 tablespoon sugar and 1/2 cup (120 mL) sour cream

Key Lime Pie

serves 6-8

This is another old recipe from my school days that resurfaced after Nico's grandmother told us how much she loves Key Lime Pie. How does a very French lady come to love Key lime pie? She lived with her husband in Florida for many years. This is a really easy recipe to make, and most of the ingredients can be found in your pantry, so this can be your staple emergency dessert.

1. Preheat oven to 350ºF (180ºC). Mix first four ingredients to create graham cracker crust. Press graham cracker mixture into a standard pie pan in an even layer.
2. Blend remaining ingredients. Pour into crust.
3. Bake for 5-15 minutes. Do not brown, wait for little bubbles to form and for the mixture to set.
4. Cool completely, for at least two hours, before serving.
5. I garnish mine with freshly made whipped cream and raspberries. Whip heavy whipping cream until soft peaks form, add a teaspoon of vanilla and sugar to taste.

graham cracker crust:

1 1/2 cup (150 g) graham crackers, ground

1/3 cup (70 g) sugar

6 tablespoons unsalted butter, melted

pinch of salt

filling:

2 14 unce (415 mL) cans sweetened condensed milk

3/4 cup (180 mL) sour cream

3/4 cup (180 mL) key lime juice or lime juice if you can't find it

1-2 teaspoons lime zest

Love Stories
Dinners for Two

The following are intimate meals that Nico and I have shared together. These are structured as two to three course meals but are meant to serve two, generally with some leftovers. One day Nico told me that a friend of his asked how he was eating in America, since we have a fairly bad culinary reputation in the rest of the world. Nico told his friend that he has never eaten better! That is one of my favorite compliments.

Filet Mignon and Balsamic Onion Jam Crostini
Valentines Day

Filet Mignon seems to be the official Valentine's Day dish! I didn't want to go the traditional Valentine's route and decided to let Red Snapper be the star of our dinner. We grilled our fillet mignon and sliced it to create a deconstructed crostini with a sweet Balsamic Onion Jam and a zesty Horseradish Crème. I served these deconstructed to create a Spanish Tapas type presentation. The combination is delicious!

1. Heat oil and butter in saucepan. Add onions, sauté 10 minutes. Stir in vinegar, sugar, and raisins. Reduce heat and cook 20 minutes, stirring occasionally until it reduces to a jam like consistency.
2. Prepare grill. Season steaks with salt and pepper and brush with oil. Rest 15 minutes. Grill steaks about 10 minutes for medium rare. Flip several times. Rest 3-5 minutes before slicing into 1/4 inch (6 mm) slices.
3. Combine all horseradish crème ingredients, season with salt and pepper.
4. Serve with finishing salt and fresh chopped rosemary.

Cuisine: Italian

jam:
1 tablespoon unsalted butter
1 tablespoon olive oil
1 large or 2 small onions, thinly sliced
1/4 cup (60 mL) balsamic vinegar
1/4 cup (50 g) brown sugar
2 tablespoons raisins
salt and pepper

meat:
2 filet mignon
2 teaspoons olive oil
salt and pepper

crème:
1/3 cup (80 mL) sour cream or yogurt
3 tablespoons horseradish
salt and pepper

crostini:
loaf of baguette p. 145 sliced thin on a diagonal, oiled and baked until crispy rubbed with garlic after baking

Prosciutto-Wrapped Red Snapper
Valentines Day

Pink for Valentine's Day? This is the best that I can do! The fish is actually quite light to balance and follow the richer crostini. Sure this is backwards of tradition, but it still works. Be careful while eating, there are small bones.

snapper:
2 red snappers, gutted
  and scaled
4 slices of lemon
4 small rosemary branches
4 ounces (115 g) prosciutto
olive oil
salt and pepper

red snapper:
1. Preheat oven to 400°F (205°C). Season fish inside and out with salt and pepper. Stuff with herbs and lemon.
2. Wrap with overlapping slices of prosciutto and use a toothpick to secure the ham to the fish.
3. Line cookie sheet with aluminum. Drizzle olive oil on both sides of fish. Bake for about 10 minutes.

Roast Brussel Sprouts with Sautéed Bread Crumbs

brussel sprouts:
1/3 - 1/2 cup (50-75 g)
  raisins, soaked in hot
  water, drained
1/4 - 1/3 cup (60-80 mL)
  olive oil
1 1/2 pound (675 g) Brussel
  sprouts, trimmed and
  halved
4 inches (10 cm) baguette
  p. 145, crust-less,
  1/3 inch (1 cm) dice
2 cloves garlic, minced
1/4 cup (60 mL) lemon juice
salt and pepper

Brussel sprouts:
1. Preheat oven to 400°F (205°C). Line cookie sheet in aluminum.
2. Toss Brussel sprouts in oil, salt and pepper. Place cut side down and bake for 20-30 minutes.
3. Heat 1/4 cup (60 mL) olive oil, toss bread crumbs, 4 minutes.
4. Sauté garlic in 1 tablespoon olive oil, 1 minute. Add Brussel sprouts, raisins, bread crumbs, 1 minute. Add lemon juice. Taste, season with salt and pepper, and serve.

Cuisine: Spanish

Crème Brûlée
Valentines Day

1. Preheat oven to 325°F (165°C).
   Heat up cream, salt, and vanilla in a small saucepan.

2. Whip egg yolks with sugar until light and fluffy.
   Add 1/4 of the cream mixture to temper.
   Whisk to combine.
   Add remaining cream mixture and blend.
   Careful to avoid making bubbles on surface.

3. Pour into four dishes.
   Place four dishes into a large high sided cookie sheet.
   Add water to halfway up the sides of the ramekins.
   Carefully place in the oven and bake for 30-40 minutes until the centers are set.

4. Refrigerate for 2-3 hours after baking. The second set can be left in the fridge for a couple of days.

5. Add 1-2 tablespoons granulated sugar evenly over the custard surface.
   Place on heat proof surface and brûlée, or place on a cookie sheet and broil for 5-8 minutes. Watching the sugar carefully to not overcook.

6. Serve with a few fresh raspberries.

Cuisine: French

After Cannelés Bordelais, Crème Brûlée is Nico's favorite dessert. He gave me a set of proper Crème Brûlée ramekins and a torch last Christmas. In America, Crème Brûlée is served in deep, narrow ramekins. In France, the custard is presented in wide shallow dishes that give you a higher sugar crust to crème ratio. I wanted to break them out for Valentine's Day. This is a delicious and simple recipe. If you don't happen to have a butane torch, you can broil the crèmes for a few minutes to achieve the same results. This recipe makes enough custard for four shallow ramekins.

———

2 cups (480 mL) heavy cream
  or half and half
1 teaspoon vanilla
1/8 teaspoon salt
5 egg yolks
1/2 cup (100 g) sugar
  + extra for the crust
raspberries to serve

Roast Duck with Cranberry Orange Sauce

Roast Duck Dinner

1. Mix one half cranberries, honey, and 1/2 cup (120 mL) water. Cook in a small saucepan until cranberries have burst and are soft throughout.
   Strain liquid and reserve, this will be the glaze for your duck. Reserve cranberry mash for stuffing the duck.
2. Preheat oven to 350°F (180°C). Remove and reserve the inner bits of your duck.
   Replace with the skins of your juiced orange, 1/2 of the onion, and the mashed cranberry. Season duck with salt and pepper.
3. Place in a roasting pan or Dutch oven and brush on some of the reserved glaze.
4. Roast for 50 minutes.
   Every 10 minutes, open the oven and brush on more of the glaze. After 50 minutes, remove from oven and prick all over with a fork to allow fat to escape.
5. Return to oven for another hour and 10 minutes.
   Add glaze every 10 minutes.
6. While the duck is roasting, roughly chop 1/2 onion and the innards from the duck.
   Place in small sauce pan, add wine and 1 cup (240 mL) water. Season with salt and pepper.

This might be the best dish I have ever cooked! I now keep a duck in the freezer just in case of emergency! The meat itself is great, but the winner of the dinner is the sauce which is developed through several steps as the duck roasts. Another great benefit is the cup full of duck fat that you can use for other purposes. Duck fat lasts somewhere between six months and forever in the fridge!

_____

2 cups (200 g) cranberries
1/2 cup (120 mL) honey
2 cups (480 mL) water
4 pound (1.8 kg) duck
Peel and juice of one
  orange
1 onion
1/3 cup (80 mL) white wine
1/2 cup (100 g) sugar
1 tablespoon balsamic

7. Simmer until you have 1/2 cup (120mL) of liquid, about one hour. Strain.

8. In a separate saucepan, combine orange juice and water to make 1/2 cup (120 mL) of liquid. Add remaining cranberries, sugar, and balsamic vinegar. Cook for 10 minutes until syrupy.

9. Once baked, set the bird aside on a serving platter. Remove fat from roasting pan and reserve for other uses.

10. Add the innards broth to the remaining drippings in the roasting pan and deglaze. Strain the liquid and add to cranberry sauce.

11. Cook cranberry sauce to desired thickness and season if necessary.

Spaghetti Squash with Thyme and Olive Oil
Roast Duck Dinner

1 small or medium spaghetti squash
2 tablespoons (30 mL) olive oil + extra for rubbing
1 tablespoon fresh thyme
salt and pepper

1. Preheat oven to 450°F (230°C). Cut spaghetti squash in half, remove and discard seeds. Rub squash with oil and sprinkle with salt and pepper.

2. Place cut side up on cookie sheet and bake for about 40-60 minutes, depending on the size of your squash. If it is small, check after 30 minutes.
It is done when you can pierce through the whole thing with a fork. Allow to cool slightly and use a fork to scrape all of the flesh out. Season with salt and pepper, add a bit of olive oil. Sprinkle with thyme.

Cuisine: French

Raspberry Cream Cheese Cake

Roast Duck Dinner

Cream cheese frosting seems to always be reserved for red velvet or carrot cakes. I wanted to try something different. I always put raspberry on cheesecake, so I figured this would work too. This cake started as a melange of other cakes I have created to make a layer cake that Nico would enjoy. This recipe makes a three layer cake with a 6 inch (15 cm) round pan. Feel free to double the recipe to create a standard 9 inch (23 cm) round.

vanilla cake:

3/4 cup (150 g) sugar

1 1/2 cup (180 g) cake flour

1 1/2 teaspoon baking powder

1/2 teaspoon salt

8 tablespoons unsalted butter

1/2 cup (120 mL) sour cream

1 egg and 2 egg yolks

1 1/2 teaspoon vanilla

frosting:

4 tablespoons unsalted butter

16 ounces (450 g) cream
  cheese

sugar to taste

1 teaspoon vanilla

raspberry filling:

2 cups (200 g) raspberries

1/2 cup (100 g) sugar

1/2 teaspoon lemon juice

1. Preheat oven to 375°F (190°C)
   Mix all cake ingredients.
   Place in three 6 inch (25 cm) buttered tins.
   Bake until golden and set, 20 minutes or so.
   Remove and cool.
2. Beat cream cheese and butter until fluffy.
   Add sugar and vanilla.
3. Cook berries, lemon, and sugar until syrupy.
   Allow to cool.
4. Assemble: cake, cream cheese, jam, repeat.
   Reserve some cream cheese for frosting the exterior.
   Serve with fresh raspberries.

Cuisine: American

Pan con Tomate and Gazpacho
Spanish Tapas

We spent New Years in Spain last year. We went for the amazing Moorish architecture but were inspired by the delicious meals. In many restaurants, you receive a free snack with every glass of wine. We feasted on fish and meats all drenched in the highest quality olive oil. This is where I learned about the power of finishing salt.

pan con tomate:

1. Broil baguettes for a few minutes until brown.
   Arrange all of the ingredients on a platter.
2. Diners should scrape some garlic on their bread and rub the tomato all over the surface. Arrange the remaining ingredients to taste.

gazpacho:

1. Blend all of the ingredients together. Season with salt and pepper.
   Allow to chill for at least four hours before serving. Serve cold.

Cuisine: Spanish

pan con tomate:

1 loaf of baguette p. 145, halved and sliced lengthwise
1 ripe tomato, sliced in half
1 clove garlic, sliced in half
slices of Manchego cheese
Kalamata olives
24 anchovies
finishing salt

gazpacho:

1 red bell pepper, diced
1 large cucumber, peeled and diced
2 pounds (900 g) very ripe tomatoes, diced
2 garlic cloves
4 inch (10 cm) piece baguette, cubed
1 tablespoon red wine vinegar
2 tablespoons dry red wine
1/2 cup (120 mL) or so olive oil
salt and pepper

Goat Cheese Custard with Fresh Mango

Spanish Tapas

The mint essence in this custard is really delicious and light. It will pair well with fresh fruit of any kind, but we had a couple of mangoes on hand so I went with them. We tried the leftovers with an apricot-peach jam. That combination worked as well, but we preferred the less sugary fresh fruit option. The recipe makes six servings, but the custards last a couple of days in the fridge.

1 1/4 cup (300 mL) whole milk or half and half
1 packet, or 1 tablespoon (9 g) unsweetened gelatin
3 1/4 cups (780 mL) heavy cream
big handful fresh mint leaves
11 ounces (300 g) goat cheese
1/3 cup (80 mL) honey + extra to drizzle
1/8 teaspoon salt
cubed fresh mango
ice cubes

1. Hydrate gelatin in a small pot with milk.
2. Boil mint and cream together. Let stand for five minutes.
   Strain out and discard mint leaves right before step 5.
3. Crumble goat cheese into a large bowl.
4. Heat milk and gelatin until the gelatin dissolves. Remove from heat.
   Add honey and salt.
5. Combine with cream mixture and gelatin milk.
   Pour over goat cheese. Whisk until perfectly smooth.
6. Pour through a fine mesh to separate any leftover chunks.
7. Prepare large bowl with ice and water.
   Place a smaller bowl holding the custard mixture within the ice bath.
   Mix the custard constantly until the consistency becomes thicker.
8. Divide into 6 serving dishes and refrigerate for 8 hours to 1 day.
   Serve with fresh chopped mango and honey drizzled on top.

Cuisine: Spanish

Kubaneh

Cajun with a Twist

1. Mix water and yeast in stand mixer or bowl. Add flour, sugar, and salt. Mix to combine.
2. Knead until evenly blended.
3. Knead by hand for 3-5 minutes until uniform ball shape is formed.
4. Let dough rest and rise for 30 minutes in a covered oiled bowl.
5. Melt butter. Spread 1 tablespoon butter on large plate.
   Divide the dough into 8 equal pieces and shape into balls.
   Place on buttered plate and smear a bit more butter.
   Cover and rest for 30 minutes.
5. Butter a clean work counter.
   Take one ball at a time, flatten it, add a tablespoon of butter and roll it out into about a 12 inch (30 cm) square. Fold into three parts like a letter, 4x12 inch (10x30 cm). Roll into a cigar (4 in/10 cm long, about 2 in/5 cm in circumference). Cut the cigar into two short columns, 2x2 inch (5x5 cm). Repeat.
6. Butter a spring form pan and arrange cigars, cut side up.
   Butter the tops of the cigars.
   Cover in plastic wrap and let rise for one hour in a cold oven with a pilot light on.
7. Cover the bottom of the spring form in aluminum foil.
   Preheat oven to 350°F (180°C).
8. Bake for 10 minutes. Turn heat to 325°F (180°C) for 30-40 minutes.

Cuisine: Yemenite

This is in no way a Cajun dish, neither of French nor Southern in origin. Kubaneh is a Yemenite bread that I came across once and immediately latched onto. I was in the midst of attempts at croissants at the time and the relative simplicity of this bread was a welcome respite. I loved the presentation, like a bouquet of flowers. This dish takes a bit of patience but it is delicious and is a great accompaniment to any soup. Traditionally it would be served with grated tomato.

———

1 1/4 cup (300 mL) water

2 1/4 teaspoons (8 g) active dry yeast

4 cups (480 g) bread flour

1/4 cup sugar

1 rounded tablespoon (20 g) salt

10 tablespoons unsalted butter, softened

Cajun Shrimp Soup

Cajun with a Twist

The basis of Cajun cooking is a roux. The roux is a cooked fat and flour mixture. The French version calls for butter, while the Cajun calls for oil. I couldn't decide so I use both. If you want to create a proper roux, make a larger quantity and keep stirring on low heat for 40 minutes to an hour. The small batch allows for a quicker brown, but surely loses a bit of the smoky flavor. After the roux, we incorporate the holy trinity of Cajun cooking: onion, celery, and bell pepper. I add a some garlic and chili pepper.

1. Heat oil and butter.
    Add flour to make a quick roux by stirring on low heat for about 10-15 minutes until browned.
2. Add celery, bell pepper, green onions, garlic, and onion.
    Cook until softened, about 10 minutes.
3. Add in corn, broth, tomatoes, paprika, and bay leaves.
    Simmer for 30 minutes.
4. Add shrimp and parsley, reserving some parsley to garnish.
    Cook for 5 minutes until shrimp is cooked through.
    Season with salt and pepper.

2 tablespoons flour
1 tablespoon olive oil
1 tablespoon butter
3 stems celery, chopped
1/2 red or green bell
  pepper, chopped
2 green onions, chopped
1 onion, chopped
2 cloves garlic, minced
3 14 ounce (415 mL) cans
  creamed corn, with liquid
1 can corn kernels, drained
1 14 ounce can (415 mL)
  diced tomatoes
2-3 cups (480-720 mL) fish
  broth
2 bay leaves
1 1/2 teaspoon paprika
1 pound cleaned shrimp
large handful fresh parsley,
  chopped
salt and pepper

Cuisine: Cajun

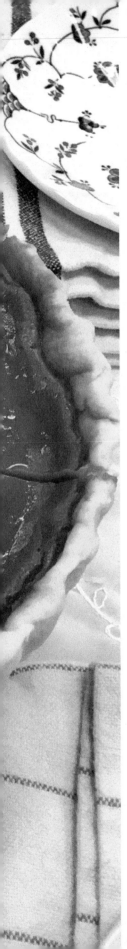

Cranberry Orange Tart

Cajun with a Twist

1. Mix softened butter and flour together, by hand.
    Add salt, sugar, and a bit of water to bring it together into a ball.
    You want pieces of butter left in the dough, an overworked dough will become very tough once baked.
2. Chill for a half an hour.
3. Preheat oven to 400°F (205°C)
    Roll crust out to fit into an 8 inch (20 cm) tart pan.
    Line with parchment. Add a layer of baking beans.
    Bake for 20 minutes or so.
4. Cook orange juice, zest, cranberry, and sugar for 10 minutes.
    Puree. Add butter.
2. Lower heat to 350°F (180°C)
    Separately, mix together eggs and egg yolks. Add a bit of cranberry mixture to temper.
    Add the egg mixture to the rest of the cranberry mixture.
3. Pour mixture into tart shell and bake for 15 minutes until set.

Cuisine: French

Cajun cuisine pulls a lot from French cuisine, incorporating different flavors and spices to make the dishes new. The tarte au citron is the inspiration for this dish. We had cranberries left over from one of the other dinners, and I wanted to make use of them before they went bad. I figured the buttery bread and hearty soup could use a finish that had a bit more of a fresh tang.

———

crust:

12 tablespoons unsalted butter

2 cups (240 g) cake flour

4-6 tablespoons cold water

4 tablespoons sugar

1 teaspoon salt

filling:

12 ounces (350 g) cranberries

1 cup (200 g) sugar

juice and zest of 1 orange

8 tablespoons unsalted butter

2 eggs and 2 egg yolks

Three's Company
dinners for curated guests

I am not always entertaining large groups. Sometimes a friend or two are in town, or my parents visit for the weekend. These menus are ones I created for smaller groups of visitors. They are generally handled the day-of, so no need for days of preparation the way the other dinners require. A few hour's notice should be enough to prepare all of these dishes. For the most part, these meals are two to three course dinners, but feel free to pick and choose dishes from various parts of this book to complete your meal. I have listed where these dishes come from so you can mix and match.

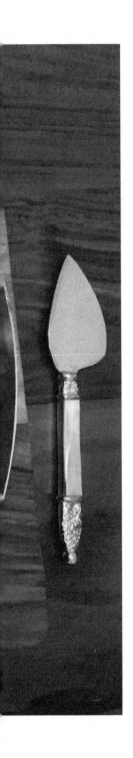

Baked Camembert with Porcini and Figs

Lapin Bourguignon

I am not a huge fan of Brie for a cheese for a cheese plate. However, I do enjoy baking it. Brie and Camembert work really well when paired with jams and pastry. I like to make a version of this with a red berry and walnuts sealed in a puff pastry. This version pairs porcini mushrooms with balsamic vinegar and figs.

1 pound (450 g) Camembert
2 tablespoons unsalted butter
1 tablespoon olive oil
3 large shallots, sliced
2 cups (150 g) porcini
  mushrooms
salt and pepper
1 teaspoon fresh thyme
1/2 cup to 2/3 cup
  (120-180 mL) fig jam
water to thin

1. Preheat oven to 400°F (205°C).
2. Sauté shallot in butter and oil. Cook for 3 minutes.
   Add mushrooms, thyme, salt, and pepper and sauté for 8-10 minutes.
3. Add fig jam and sauté for a few minutes longer.
   Add a bit water if it is getting too thin.
4. Place cheese in oven proof dish. Arrange topping around cheese, bake for 8-10 minutes.
5. Slice up baguette, brush with oil and broil for a few minutes.

Cuisine: French

Celery Velouté with Bacon
and Duck Fat Croutons

Lapin Bourguignon

celery velouté:

1. Heat butter in large Dutch oven. Sauté onions for 5-7 minutes. Add garlic, sauté for 2 additional minutes. Add celery, season with salt and pepper.
2. Add chicken broth concentrate and sauté for twenty minutes.
3. Add milk and or cream. Bring to boil, lower and cook for 30 minutes on low simmer.
4. Add parsley and mix.
5. Blend with an immersion blender until completely smooth. Add water or more milk if the soup is too thick. Season with salt and pepper.
7. Serve with Bacon Croutons and reserved celery leaves as garnish.

duck fat croutons:

1. Heat butter in cast iron skillet.
2. Add bacon and cook for 5-7 minutes, until crispy.
3. Add bread cubes and cook, stirring constantly, for about 5 minutes until the fat is absorbed and the croutons are crispy.
4. Season with salt and pepper.

Cuisine: French

Velouté denotes a velvety smooth texture. This dish is definitely smooth like velvet. I had some extra celery and thought this dish would make good use of it. A mixture of milk and cream makes for a very rich dish. I wouldn't serve a whole bowl of this, but it is amazing in small quantities! The bacon and duck fat croutons add a smoky touch.

———

celery velouté:

4 tablespoons butter
2 onions, diced
3 cloves garlic, thinly sliced
1/2 pound, thinly sliced
   celery, reserve inner leaves
1 teaspoon chicken broth
   concentrate
4 cups (450 g) half and half
1/2 bunch parsley leaves
1/8 teaspoon paprika
salt and pepper

croutons:

4 inches (10 cm) baguette,
   1/3 inch (1 cm) cube
3-4 slices finely diced bacon
1 tablespoon unsalted butter
salt and pepper

207

Lapin Bourguignon with Porcini Mushrooms

Lapin Bourguignon

On our first semi-official date, Nico and I made Lapin au Moutarde together. The rabbit was a bit tough, but it was a lovely way to spend time together. One of Nico's friends was in town and I wanted to revisit the rabbit, but with a recipe I was really sure of. This is how Lapin Bourguignon came about. Generally, the dish is served with white button mushrooms, but I figured porcini would pair well with the gamey nature of rabbit, and it gave me the opportunity to use mushroom broth with the wine. Make a day ahead for a more complex flavor. Serve with pasta, potatoes, or rice.

1 rabbit, cut into parts (reference YouTube for help)

1/2 cup (120 mL) olive oil

2 tablespoons butter

2 tablespoons all purpose flour

1/2 cup (120 mL) cognac or brandy

2 onions, finely chopped

5 garlic cloves, minced

1/2 cup (115 g) bacon, chopped small

1 tablespoon tomato paste

2-3 sprigs thyme

1 sprig laurel

1 bottle dry red wine from Burgundy

3 carrots, sliced

2 cups porcini mushrooms

2 cups mushroom broth, from re-hydrating dried porcini mushrooms

1. Heat oil and butter in large Dutch oven. Brown rabbit until lightly colored. Add flour, stir.
2. Deglaze with brandy or cognac.
3. Add onions and garlic, 3 minutes. Add bacon, 5 minutes. Scrape. Add tomato paste, stir. Add herbs, tie together with string.
4. Cover rabbit completely with red wine and mushroom broth. Boil. Add carrots, reduce to simmer. Cover and cook 2 hours.
5. Separate liquid. Add half onions, carrot, bacon to liquid. Blend.
6. Fry the mushrooms in butter. Put everything back together.

Cuisine: French

Coq au Vin
Coq au Vin

1. Rub chicken with salt and pepper. Place in large bowl. Add 1 onion, carrot, herbs, wine, and bay leaf. Cover and chill overnight.
2. Remove and dry chicken. Strain marinade, reserve all.
3. Heat 1 tablespoon (15 ml) oil and 1 tablespoon (15 g) butter. Add bacon, 6-8 minutes. Set aside.
4. Brown chicken, skin sides down. Remove all but 3 tablespoons (45 mL) of fat. Cook the mushrooms, 8-10 minutes. Set aside.
5. Cook reserved aromatics, 8-10 minutes. Stir in flour, mix. Return chicken back to pan.
6. Pour in wine to cover chicken. Add some water if needed. Simmer for 30-40 minutes.
8. Separately, heat remaining fat and brown onions, 8-10 minutes. Season and add water to cover. Cook 15-20 minutes. Remove chicken, add vinegar, cook 10 minutes.
   Add chicken, mushrooms, bacon, and cooked onions, serve.

Cuisine: French

When I was a student I would always buy chicken legs and stew them in a large pot for a week's worth of dinners. Back then, I would buy $2 wine from Trader Joe's. I have since upgraded to a decent-ish bottle of Burgundy. Like Bourguignon, Coq au Vin is great with pasta (p. 223), rice, or potato and a nice loaf of baguette (p. 145).

------

1 chicken, chopped or 2 pounds (900 g) chicken legs
6-7 ounces (200 g) bacon
1 bottle of red, Burgundy
4 tablespoons unsalted butter
2 onions, chopped
2 cloves garlic, minced
thyme, parsley, laurel, bouquet tied with string
16 ounces (900 g) mushrooms
bay leaf
2 large carrots, chopped
1 tablespoon flour
3 tablespoons oil
1 tablespoon red wine vinegar

Chocolate Caramel Tart
Coq au Vin

1. Mix flour and cocoa together. Mix softened butter and flour together, by hand. Add salt and enough water to make rough ball.
2. Chill for a half an hour.
3. Preheat oven to 400°F (205°C). Roll crust into an 10 inch (25 cm) tart pan. Line with parchment. Add a layer of baking beans. Bake for 10 minutes or so. Remove beans, bake 10 minutes.
4. Bring water and sugar to boil. Cook for 10-15 minutes until caramel forms, do not stir. Remove from heat and whisk in butter, heavy cream and salt. Whisk until smooth.
5. Pour into tart shell and leave to cool and set for 1 hour.
6. Place chocolate in a bowl. Bring cream to a boil. Pour over chocolate, whisk until smooth. Pour over caramel. Refrigerate 1 hour. Sprinkle fleur de sel.

I don't usually like caramel, but I do like Bouchees au Caramel, a chewy soft caramel square from France sprinkled with Fleur de Sel. I saw a recipe for a caramel chocolate pie online once, now I can't find it so I combined a few different ones to make this dish. It is perfect in small quantities. It is very dense. Sprinkle on the Fleur de Sel right before serving.

———

crust:
12 tablespoons unsalted butter
2 cups (240 g) cake flour
4-6 tablespoons cold water
6 tablespoons cocoa powder
1 teaspoon salt

filling:
2 1/4 cups (450 g) sugar
1/2 cup (120 mL) water
8 tablespoons unsalted butter
1/2 cup (120 mL) heavy cream
pinch of salt

chocolate ganache:
4 ounces (115 g) dark chocolate
1/2 cup (120 mL) heavy cream
fleur de sel

Cuisine: French

Crab Cakes
Crab Cake Dinner

Crab cakes are a Baltimore staple. Every time a new friend comes to visit, we feel like we should take them out for crab cakes. It is an expensive endeavor to do right. After a while, I figured I should just start making my own. They can be served on any kind of bread, but I like the ones we made with homemade focaccia rolls. Just divide the focaccia dough (p. 109) into roll size balls. Serve with any of the salads you find in this book, and some quintessentially American dessert like Key lime Pie (p. 177), Cheesecake (p. 175), or Blueberry Pie (p. 91).

crab cakes:

1 pound (450 g) crab meat

2 tablespoons breadcrumbs

1 tablespoon chopped
  parsley

1 egg, beaten

1 1/2 tablespoon
  mayonnaise

1 tablespoon mustard

1/2 teaspoon paprika

salt and pepper

to serve:

4 focaccia rolls

tartar sauce, to serve

1 cup (20 g) arugula

1.   Mix all ingredients. Divide into four patties.
      Preheat broiler.
2.   Line cookie sheet with parchment and arrange patties.
      Broil for 12-15 minutes, flipping halfway through.
      Watch carefully, if they brown too quickly, switch and bake at 350°F (180°C) for 10 minutes.
3.   To serve, add a bit of tartar on the bun, add some arugula, and a crab cake.

Cuisine: American

Challah French Toast
and Bad Milk Pancakes
Saturday Brunch

Sometimes I make Challah just to make it into French Toast. Nico and I eat French Toast or Pancakes almost every weekend. I like to use Cinnamon Raisin Challah to make this dish. Use Challah recipe (p. 32). When forming the braids, flatten them like baguette dough. Sprinkle with a mixture of sugar and cinnamon and sprinkle raisins before rolling up, pinching sealed, and braiding into a loaf as usual. The pancakes are my go-to recipe when I need to use up spoiled milk. My mom used to make us pancakes whenever the milk went bad when I was a kid. I learned it from her.

French toast:

1. Cut 6 slices of Challah.
2. Mix all ingredients together. Dip slices of challah until well absorbed.
3. Fry in butter until golden.
4. Serve with syrup or raspberry jam.

bad milk pancakes:

1. Mix all ingredients. Add enough bad milk, or buttermilk if you have it, to get to a consistency you like.
2. Heat some butter or oil on skillet. Fry until bubbles form. Flip.
3. Serve with jams or syrup.

Cuisine: American

French toast:

6 thick slices of Challah
   Bread, p. 32
4 eggs
1 1/2 cup (360 mL) milk
1/3 cup (70 g) sugar
1 teaspoon vanilla
pinch of salt

bad milk pancakes:

1 cup (120 g) all purpose
   flour
2 eggs
2 tablespoons olive oil
   or melted butter
1 teaspoon baking soda
2 teaspoons baking powder
1 teaspoon vanilla
enough bad milk to desired
   consistency
pinch of salt

Weeknight Dinners

We have different schedules during the week. I get up at 6 am to get to work, and Nico comes back around 8:30 pm or later. Weeknight dinners become very important to us because these are some of our only bits of time to spend together during the week.

French Onion Soup and Anchovy Butter

serves 6

What a great way to use up a bunch of onions that are close to death! This recipe also happens to be a good way to use up bread that is a bit too stale and cheese that isn't large enough for a cheese plate. This is a lovely recipe and is quite easy to make.

onion soup:

1. Melt 3 tablespoons of butter in a large Dutch oven.
Add oil and onions.
Sauté for 15 minutes.
2. Season with salt and pepper and sauté until onions have browned, 30 minutes.
3. Add wine and cook until almost dry, 15-20 minutes.
4. Add broth, herbs, and simmer for 20-30 minutes until thickened.
Add 2 tablespoons butter.
5. Heat broiler and crisp up bread. You want it dried not browned. Rub one side with a bit of garlic.
6. Pour soup into ramekins, add garlic toast, sprinkle with cheese. Broil until melted and bubbly.

anchovy butter:

1. Soften butter, mix all ingredients together. Serve with toast.

Cuisine: French

onion soup:

5 tablespoons unsalted butter, separated

1 tablespoon olive oil

4-5 large onions

1/2 teaspoon sugar

1 1/2 cup (360 mL) dry white wine

6 cups (1.5 L) beef broth

handful of sprigs of thyme and 2 bay leaves, tied with string

crusty bread, sliced to fit ramekins

1 clove garlic, cut in half

2 teaspoons sherry or vermouth

4 ounces (115 g) Gruyère, grated

salt and pepper

anchovy butter:

8 tablespoons unsalted butter

1 pack anchovies, drained

3 cloves garlic, minced

pinch of paprika

splash of lemon juice

salt and pepper

Pasta or Polenta with Eggplant Sauce

serves 2 -4 generously

fresh pasta:

1. Place flour in volcano shape. Add salt and eggs to crater. Mix until ball forms, add water if needed.
2. Knead 5 minutes. Form into tennis sized balls.
3. Dust pasta machine with flour and pull dough through, folding like a letter after each pass. Make setting smaller, to desired thickness, roll through final time. Trim to 12 inch pieces and cover.
4. Repeat with remainder.
5. Run through cutting roller. Dust with flour to separate.
6. Boil water. Cook 2-3 minutes.

sauce:

1. Sauté onions and garlic in olive oil, 5 minutes. Add eggplant and cook until browned, 15 minutes.
2. Add tomato paste, stir 1 minute. Add tomatoes, wine and spices. Season with salt and pepper, cook until thickened. Serve with fresh grated Parmesan.

fresh corn polenta:

1. Place corn kernels in pan, cover with water. Simmer for 12 minutes. Drain, reserving the water.
2. Process cooked kernels in blender.
3. Return to pot, add 1/2 corn water, cook 10-15 minutes. Add butter, feta, season with salt and pepper, add more corn water if needed.

Cuisine: Italian

This dish is so much fun to make. Rolling pasta through a press is totally therapeutic and the mixture of eggplant and tomato is a delicious topping for your efforts.

———

pasta:

4 cups (480 g) flour

6 eggs

8 tablespoons unsalted butter

salt and pepper

sauce:

olive oil

3 cloves garlic, minced

1 small onion, finely chopped

2 tablespoons tomato paste

4 small eggplant, finely chopped

3 medium tomatoes, finely chopped

1 cup (240 mL) white wine

4 sprigs thyme

3 sprigs oregano

salt and pepper

fresh polenta:

6 ears corn, kernels cut off

2 1/4 cups (540 mL) water

3 tablespoons unsalted butter

7 ounces (200 g) feta

Salmon and Horseradish Crème
with Légumes-Racines Rôtis au Four

serves 2 generously

We have been trying to eat a bit less meat and have been cooking a lot of vegetables and salmon. This gave me a great opportunity to explore various toppings for fish and paired roasting sauces for the vegetables.

salmon with horseradish crème:

1. Heat oven to 350°F (180°C). Heat pan to very hot. Add oil. Add seasoned salmon. Sear for 3 minutes.
2. Add butter. Baste for 1 minute. Flip, keep basting for 2 more minutes.
3. Place in oven until cooked through, 5-9 more minutes.
4. Mix all horseradish crème ingredients. Season with salt and pepper.

légumes-racines rôtis au four:

1. Preheat oven to 400°F (205°C). Cut vegetables to bite sized pieces. Toss in oil, season with salt and pepper. Spread on baking sheet and bake for 25-35 minutes.
2. Simmer vinegar, sugar, and salt. Add orange juice. Cook for 10-15 minutes for maple syrup consistency.
3. Melt butter in saucepan. Add vegetables and caraway seeds. Add glaze, toss to coat.

roast acorn squash with fennel:

1. Preheat oven to 450°F (230°C). Mix all ingredients. Bake for 45 minutes. Serve with Cilantro Chutney, p. 43.

Cuisine: French and Indian

seared salmon:
2 salmon fillets
salt and pepper
2 teaspoons olive oil
1 tablespoon unsalted butter

horseradish crème:
1/3 cup (80 mL) sour cream
1-2 teaspoons horseradish
2 teaspoons minced parsley
1 teaspoon lemon zest

légumes-racines rôtis au four:
2-3 pounds (1 - 1.5 kg)
   root vegetables
4 tablespoons olive oil
3 tablespoons unsalted butter
2 teaspoons caraway seeds
salt and pepper

glaze:
2/3 cup (160 mL) sherry vinegar
1/2 cup (100 g) sugar
1/4 cup (60 mL) orange juice
salt and pepper

roast acorn squash with fennel:
2 acorn squash, sliced
   along ridges
2 fennel bulbs, trimmed,
   cut into wedges
2 large onions, wedges
1/4 cup (60 mL) olive oil
2 teaspoons cumin
2 teaspoons cinnamon
1/2 teaspoon paprika
1 teaspoon turmeric
salt and pepper

Sautéed Leek and Chèvre Grilled Cheese and Roast Summer Squash with Fennel

serves 2 generously

I love grilled cheese sandwiches but I hate the idea of orange cheese so I like to change it up. There is so much variety with a grilled cheese. Fennel and Fontina, Pesto, Tomato, and Mozzarella, or Fennel Pesto and Goat Cheese all sound delicious. This recipe is for sautéed leek and goat cheese.

grilled cheese:

1. Heat oil in frying pan. Sauté leek for 10 minutes until softened. Season and sprinkle with thyme. Cook for another 2 minutes. Add white vinegar and reduce for 1 more minute.
2. Spread some goat cheese on each piece of bread. Divide the leek mixture and top with second bread.
3. Heat butter in frying pan. Grill for 4 minutes per side until golden.

summer squash with fennel:

1. Preheat oven to 450°F (230°C). Combine all but garlic and spread on parchment lined cookie sheet. Bake for 10 minutes.
2. Add garlic, bake for an additional 5-10 minutes.
3. Splash white wine vinegar to serve.

Cuisine: Italian

grilled cheese:

4 slices of sourdough or rustic bread

2 tablespoons unsalted butter

1 teaspoon fresh thyme

1 tablespoon olive oil

1 leek, white part sliced

1 teaspoon white wine vinegar

6 tablespoons chèvre

salt and pepper

summer squash with fennel:

3-4 summer squash, quartered 1 inch (2.5 cm) slice

2 heads fennel, sliced into half rounds

2 tablespoons olive oil

1 teaspoon thyme

1 tablespoon rosemary, chopped

1 head garlic, cloves thinly sliced

1-2 tablespoons white wine vinegar

Sweet Potato Curry Soup

serves 4-6

Nico loves soup so I have been making a lot more of them over the past few years. I love eating Naan and other breads, so soup feels like a great vehicle for carbohydrates. Yes, I am admitting to dipping my bread in soup. This is a good use for sweet potatoes when they become really cheap at the market.

2 pounds (900 g) sweet potatoes

4 teaspoons olive oil

2 small onions, chopped

3 inch (8 cm) piece of ginger, minced

3-4 cloves garlic, minced

1/2 teaspoon cumin

1/2 teaspoon paprika

1/4 teaspoon turmeric

1/4 teaspoon garam masala

1/4 teaspoon coriander

1 16 ounce (480 mL) can coconut milk

4-6 cups (1-1.5 L) chicken stock

1. Preheat oven to 400°F (205°C). Peel and chop sweet potatoes. Bake for 20 minutes until soft.
2. Heat oil in Dutch oven. Add garlic and ginger, 2 minutes. Add all spices, 2 minutes. Add onions, 5 minutes.
3. Add broth and coconut milk. Season with salt and pepper. Boil, reduce heat, simmer for a few minutes.
4. Add sweet potatoes and a bit of lemon juice. Simmer for 10 minutes or so.
5. Purée, add some water if needed.
6. Serve with cilantro and Naan, p. 53.

Cuisine: Indian

Rustic Tomato Braised Chicken

serves 4-6

This is another of my Coq au Vin variations from my student days. White wine and crushed tomatoes pair well with fennel seeds in the broth.

1. Cook bacon in Dutch oven, 4 minutes.
   Remove and drain out most of the oil.
2. Season chicken and brown on all sides.
3. Drain of all but 2 tablespoons of fat. Add onion and cook until softened, 8-10 minutes.
4. Add garlic, thyme, fennel seeds, pepper and bay leaf.
   Cook 1 minute.
5. Add white wine, boil for 2 minutes.
   Add tomatoes and stir together.
6. Add chicken and bacon back to tomato mixture.
   Simmer on low heat for about an hour until chicken is cooked through.
7. Serve with pasta or rice or add 1 cup (200 g) of lentils, 1 cup (240 mL) wine, and 1 cup (240 mL) water and cook 30-40 minutes longer.

Cuisine: French

4 slices bacon, chopped

1 large onion, thinly sliced

4 cloves garlic, minced

1 teaspoon thyme

1 teaspoon fennel seeds

1 teaspoon pepper

1 bay leaf

1 cup (240 mL) dry white wine

1 28 ounce (830 mL) can of crushed tomatoes

1 teaspoon salt

10 bone in chicken thighs

large handful chopped parsley

Acknowledgements

First, I must thank my partner and love of my life, Nicolas Charon. He has supported me through every crazy endeavor I have embarked on. He didn't bat an eyelash when I decided to completely demolish the kitchen in his newly purchased home with no prior knowledge of construction. He helped me realize the kitchen of my dreams, one that can fit our growing number of friends. He has always been our staff dishwasher and performs his duty without complaint. He does his best not to make fun of me for constantly bringing new cooking utensils home from my various adventures. He has eaten every single dish in this cookbook and has inspired the creation of most. He is also the kind of guy who would use three different emails to secretly fund your Kickstarter campaign so you wouldn't be disappointed with your success. I love this man.

A huge thank you also to Gonzo Beck, who has been here from the start! It is his shared love for cooking that inspired me to keep going with Chez Nous despite us being the only remaining founding members of our little club. He is an amazing cook and is responsible for many dishes for our dinners. You will have to seek him out for his recipes! Thank you Gonzo!

I am indebted to my best friend, Rafael Soldi, for inspiring me with his incredible entrepreneurism to strike out on my own and make this happen! He is also responsible for the amazing portrait of me in the intro chapter and taught me how to cook Peruvian food for our Peru chapter. Rafael Soldi also benevolently volunteered to be the lead editor for this book.

Where would I be without all of the amazing friends and strangers who have come to dinner, tasted my recipes, tested my recipes in their own kitchens, and inspired me to continue with my journey? Nowhere! So thank you Terry and Neil Shovlin, Paul Escande and Lisa Lafeuillade, Valentin Leroy, Khalid Ali, Keith Rama and Jacqueline Soto, Joe Cypressi, Prashant Athavale and Lucy Lee, Teresa Ertel and the whole Ertel family, Lake Newton, Mohamed Farid, Marie Tosto, Jade Wheeler, Sara Cluggish, Romain and Vanessa Nardou, Martha Kent Martin, Tahdiul Haq, Bridget Sunderlin, Rachel Valsing, Mike and Joanne Bare, and Manda Remmen.

Who else made this possible? The 76 amazing people who helped fund my Kickstarter to self-publish the first edition of this book! I am especially grateful to Nicolas Charon, Isabelle and Pierre Charon, Ivan Souvorov, George Billis, Rafael Soldi, Molly Dill, Alexander Souvorov and Katerina Souvorova, and Omead Afshari for your generous contributions! Big thank you also to everyone who purchased their copy of the cookbook before it even existed: Ana Vizcarra Rankin, Edward Mudd, Linda McConaughy, Romain Nardou, Christopher Blum, James Morrison, Fori McLean, Aurele Turnes, Jennifer G Erickson, Laura Laubenthal & Erik Genalo, Jackeline Soto, James Bryan, Elizabeth Hudson, Irene Iwasaka, Gunes Orman, Mary Beth Loup, Paul Escande, Martin Bauer, Siri Ming, Meg Sussman, Rebecca Mlinek, Liberty Grayek, Sebastian Lange, Meghan McCall, Leslie Aguila, Matthew Clark, Linda Popp, Jacintha Clark, Brian Starnes, Nancy Bea Miller, Keith J Rama, Terry Shovlin, Michael Loverde, Jacob Francois, Kirsch Jones, Kiki Broderick, and Michael Dewberry.

Thank you so much to my editors: Rafael Soldi, Joshua Glassman, Nancy Bea Miller, and Gonzo Beck.

Big shout-out and thank you to Vincent Sacchetti who created the amazing video for my Kickstarter campaign!

Last but not least, thank you to my amazing family! My parents gave up their entire life in Belarus to give us a better future! They wanted us to grow up far away from polluted waters and to have an opportunity to succeed, and I hope I have been a credit to their faith. Thank you to my little brother for his faith in my cookbook, and for finally admitting that he likes my food! A huge thank you to my grandmother, whose selflessness has inspired my way of life.

Merci to all, and come by for dinner Chez Nous!

Index

Some of the recipes found here contain raw meat, eggs, or fish.
Please know that when these foods are consumed raw, there is
a risk that bacteria (which would be killed through cooking fully)
may be present. Please purchase the freshest possible produce,
dairy, and meats when serving raw foods from a reputable
grocery or marketplace. Make sure that the groceries are
refrigerated properly until they are served. Please know that
because of the chance presence of bacteria, these dishes
should not be eaten by the elderly, pregnant, young children,
or anyone else who may have a compromised immune system.
The author and all of her affiliates expressly disclaim any
responsibility for any negative effects that may result through
the use of these recipes or any other information contained in
this book.

CPSIA information can be obtained
at www.ICGtesting.com
Printed in the USA
BVOW05*0020061217
502094BV00025B/165/P